VGM Professional Resumes Series

RESUMES
FOR
COMMUNICATIONS
CAREERS

The Editors of
VGM Career Horizons

Printed on recyclable paper

VGM Career Horizons
a division of *NTC Publishing Group*
Lincolnwood, Illinois USA

Library of Congress Cataloging-in-Publication Data

Resumes for communication careers / the editors of VGM Career-
Horizons.

      P.   cm. — (VGM's professional resumes series)
  ISBN 0-8442-8546-3 (softbound) : $9.95
  1. Communication—Vocational guidance. 2. Résumés (Employment)
I. VGM Career Horizons (Firm) II. Series.
P91.6.R4 1991   90-50723
302.2'023—dc20   CIP

1995 Printing

Published by VGM Career Horizons, a division of NTC Publishing Group.
© 1991 by NTC Publishing Group, 4255 West Touhy Avenue,
Lincolnwood (Chicago), Illinois 60646-1975 U.S.A.

   4 5 6 7 8 9 VP 9 8 7 6 5 4 3

ACKNOWLEDGMENT

The editors gratefully acknowledge Jeffrey S. Johnson for his help in the writing and production of this book.

CONTENTS

Introduction

Your resume is your first impression on a prospective employer. Though you may be articulate, intelligent, and charming in person, a poor resume may prevent you from ever having the opportunity to demonstrate your interpersonal skills, because a poor resume may prevent you from ever being called for an interview. While few people have ever been hired solely on the basis of their resume, a well-written, well-organized resume can go a long way toward helping you land an interview. Your resume's main purpose is to get you that interview. The rest is up to you and the employer. If you both feel that you are right for the job and the job is right for you, chances are you will be hired.

A resume must catch the reader's attention yet still be easy to read and to the point. Resume styles have changed over the years. Today, brief and focused resumes are preferred. No longer do employers have the patience, or the time, to review several pages of solid type. A resume should be only one page long, if possible, and never more than two pages. Time is a precious commodity in today's business world and the resume that is concise and straightforward will usually be the one that gets noticed.

Let's not make the mistake, though, of assuming that writing a brief resume means that you can take less care in preparing it. A successful resume takes time and thought, and if you are willing to make the effort, the rewards are well worth it. Think of your resume as a sales tool with the product being you. You want to sell yourself to a prospective employer. This book is designed to help you prepare a resume that will help you further your career—to land that next job, or first job, or to return to the work force after years of absence. So, read on. Make the effort and reap the rewards that a strong resume can bring to your career. Let's get to it!

Chapter One

THE ELEMENTS OF A GOOD RESUME

A winning resume is made of the elements that employers are most interested in seeing when reviewing a job applicant. These basic elements are the essential ingredients of a successful resume and become the actual sections of your resume. The following is a list of elements that may be used in a resume. Some are essential; some are optional. We will be discussing these in this chapter in order to give you a better understanding of each element's role in the makeup of your resume:

1. Heading
2. Objective
3. Work Experience
4. Education
5. Honors
6. Activities
7. Certificates and Licenses
8. Professional Memberships
9. Special Skills
10. Personal Information
11. References

The first step in preparing your resume is to gather together information about yourself and your past accomplishments. Later you will refine this information, rewrite it in the most effective language, and organize it into the most attractive layout. First, let's take a look at each of these important elements individually.

Heading

The heading may seem to be a simple enough element in your resume, but be careful not to take it lightly. The heading should be placed at the top of your resume and should include your name, home address, and telephone numbers. If you can take calls at your current place of business, include your business number, since most employers will attempt to contact you during the business day. If this is not possible, or if you can afford it, purchase an answering machine that allows you to retrieve your messages while you are away from home. This way you can make sure you don't miss important phone calls. *Always* include your phone number on your resume. It is crucial that when prospective employers need to have immediate contact with you, they can.

Objective

When seeking a particular career path, it is important to list a job objective on your resume. This statement helps employers know the direction that you see yourself heading, so that they can determine whether your goals are in line with the position available. The objective is normally one sentence long and describes your employment goals clearly and concisely. See the sample resumes in this book for examples of objective statements.

The job objective will vary depending on the type of person you are, the field you are in, and the type of goals you have. It can be either specific or general, but it should always be to the point.

In some cases, this element is not necessary, but usually it is a good idea to include your objective. It gives your possible future employer an idea of where you are coming from and where you want to go.

The objective statement is better left out, however, if you are uncertain of the exact title of the job you seek. In such a case, the inclusion of an overly specific objective statement could result in your not being considered for a variety of acceptable positions; you should be sure to incorporate this information in your cover letter, instead.

Work Experience

This element is arguably the most important of them all. It will provide the central focus of your resume, so it is necessary that this section be as complete as possible. Only by examining your work experience in depth can you get to the heart of your accomplishments and present them in a way that demonstrates the strength of your qualifications. Of course, someone just out of school will have less work experience than someone who has been working for a number of years, but the amount of information isn't the most important thing—rather, how it is presented and how it highlights you as a person and as a worker will be what counts.

As you work on this section of your resume, be aware of the need for accuracy. You'll want to include all necessary information about each of your jobs, including job title, dates, employer, city, state, responsibilities, special projects, and accomplishments. Be sure to only list company accomplishments for which you were directly responsible. If you haven't participated in any special projects, that's all right—this area may not be relevant to certain jobs.

The most common way to list your work experience is in *reverse chronological order*. In other words, start with your most recent job and work your way backwards. This way your prospective employer sees your current (and often most important) job before seeing your past jobs. Your most recent position, if the most important, should also be the one that includes the most information, as compared to your previous positions. If you are just out of school, show your summer employment and part-time work, though in this case your education will most likely be more important than your work experience.

The following worksheets will help you gather information about your past jobs.

WORK EXPERIENCE
Job One:

Job Title _____

Dates _____

Employer _____

City, State _____

Major Duties _____

_____

_____

_____

_____

_____

_____

Special Projects _____

_____

_____

_____

Accomplishments _____

_____

_____

_____

_____

_____

_____

_____

Job Two:

Job Title _____

Dates _____

Employer _____

City, State _____

Major Duties _____

_____

_____

_____

_____

_____

_____

Special Projects _____

_____

_____

_____

Accomplishments _____

_____

_____

_____

_____

_____

_____

_____

Job Three:

Job Title _____

Dates _____

Employer _____

City, State _____

Major Duties _____

_____

_____

_____

_____

_____

_____

_____

Special Projects _____

_____

_____

_____

Accomplishments _____

_____

_____

_____

_____

_____

_____

_____

_____

Job Four:

Job Title _____

Dates _____

Employer _____

City, State _____

Major Duties _____

_____

_____

_____

_____

_____

_____

Special Projects _____

_____

_____

_____

Accomplishments _____

_____

_____

_____

_____

_____

_____

_____

_____

Education

Education is the second most important element of a resume. Your educational background is often a deciding factor in an employer's decision to hire you. Be sure to stress your accomplishments in school with the same finesse that you stressed your accomplishments at work. If you are looking for your first job, your education will be your greatest asset, since your work experience will most likely be minimal. In this case, the education section becomes the most important. You will want to be sure to include any degrees or certificates you received, your major area of concentration, any honors, and any relevant activities. Again, be sure to list your most recent schooling first. If you have completed graduate-level work, begin with that and work in reverse chronological order through your undergraduate education. If you have completed an undergraduate degree, you may choose whether to list your high school experience or not. This should be done only if your high school grade-point average was well above average.

The following worksheets will help you gather information for this section of your resume. Also included are supplemental worksheets for honors and for activities. Sometimes honors and activities are listed in a section separate from education, most often near the end of the resume.

EDUCATION

School _____

Major or Area of Concentration _____

Degree _____

Date _____

School _____

Major or Area of Concentration _____

Degree _____

Date _____

Honors

Here, you should list any awards, honors, or memberships in honorary societies that you have received. Usually these are of an academic nature, but they can also be for special achievement in sports, clubs, or other school activities. Always be sure to include the name of the organization honoring you and the date(s) received. Use the worksheet below to help gather your honors information.

HONORS

Honor: _____

Awarding Organization: _____

Date(s): _____

Honor: _____

Awarding Organization: _____

Date(s): _____

Honor: _____

Awarding Organization: _____

Date(s): _____

Honor: _____

Awarding Organization: _____

Date(s): _____

Activities

You may have been active in different organizations or clubs during your years at school; often an employer will look at such involvement as evidence of initiative and dedication. Your ability to take an active role, and even a leadership role, in a group should be included on your resume. Use the worksheet provided to list your activities and accomplishments in this area. In general, you should exclude any organization the name of which indicates the race, creed, sex, age, marital status, color, or nation of origin of its members.

ACTIVITIES

Organization/Activity: _____

Accomplishments: _____

_____

_____

Organization/Activity: _____

Accomplishments: _____

_____

_____

Organization/Activity: _____

Accomplishments: _____

_____

_____

Organization/Activity: _____

Accomplishments: _____

_____

_____

As your work experience increases through the years, your school activities and honors will play less of a role in your resume, and eventually you will most likely only list your degree and any major honors you received. This is due to the fact that, as time goes by, your job performance becomes the most important element in your resume. Through time, your resume should change to reflect this.

Certificates and Licenses

The next potential element of your resume is certificates and licenses. You should list these if the job you are seeking requires them and you, of course, have acquired them. If you have applied for a license, but have not yet received it, use the phrase "application pending."

License requirements vary by state. If you have moved or you are planning to move to another state, be sure to check with the appropriate board or licensing agency in the state in which you are applying for work to be sure that you are aware of all licensing requirements.

Always be sure that all of the information you list is completely accurate. Locate copies of your licenses and certificates and check the exact date and name of the accrediting agency. Use the following worksheet to list your licenses and certificates.

CERTIFICATES AND LICENSES

Name of License: _____

Licensing Agency: _____

Date Issued: _____

Name of License: _____

Licensing Agency: _____

Date Issued: _____

Name of License: _____

Licensing Agency: _____

Date Issued: _____

Professional Memberships

Another potential element in your resume is a section listing professional memberships. Use this section to list involvement in professional associations, unions, and similar organizations. It is to your advantage to list any professional memberships that pertain to the job you are seeking. Be sure to include the dates of your involvement and whether you took part in any special activities or held any offices within the organization. Use the following worksheet to gather your information.

PROFESSIONAL MEMBERSHIPS

Name of Organization: _____

Offices Held: _____

Activities: _____

Date(s): _____

Name of Organization: _____

Offices Held: _____

Activities: _____

Date(s): _____

Name of Organization: _____

Offices Held: _____

Activities: _____

Date(s): _____

Name of Organization: _____

Offices Held: _____

Activities: _____

Date(s): _____

Special Skills

This section of your resume is set aside for mentioning any special abilities you have that could relate to the job you are seeking. This is the part of your resume where you have the opportunity to demonstrate certain talents and experiences that are not necessarily a part of your educational or work experience. Common examples include fluency in a foreign language, or knowledge of a particular computer application.

Special skills can encompass a wide range of your talents—remember to be sure that whatever skills you list relate to the type of work you are looking for.

Personal Information

Some people include "Personal" information on their resumes. This is not generally recommended, but you might wish to include it if you think that something in your personal life, such as a hobby or talent, has some bearing on the position you are seeking. This type of information is often referred to at the beginning of an interview, when it is used as an "ice breaker." Of course, personal information regarding age, marital status, race, religion, or sexual preference should never appear on any resume.

References

References are not usually listed on the resume, but a prospective employer needs to know that you have references who may be contacted if necessary. All that is necessary to include in your resume regarding references is a sentence at the bottom stating, "References are available upon request." If a prospective employer requests a list of references, be sure to have one ready. Also, check with whomever you list to see if it is all right for you to use them as a reference. Forewarn them that they may receive a call regarding a reference for you. This way they can be prepared to give you the best reference possible.

Chapter Two

WRITING YOUR RESUME

Now that you have gathered together all of the information for each of the sections of your resume, it's time to write out each section in a way that will get the attention of whoever is reviewing it. The type of language you use in your resume will affect its success. You want to take the information you have gathered and translate it into a language that will cause a potential employer to sit up and take notice.

Resume writing is not like expository writing or creative writing. It embodies a functional, direct writing style and focuses on the use of action words. By using action words in your writing, you more effectively stress past accomplishments. Action words help demonstrate your initiative and highlight your talents. Always use verbs that show strength and reflect the qualities of a "doer." By using action words, you characterize yourself as a person who takes action, and this will impress potential employers.

The following is a list of verbs commonly used in resume writing. Use this list to choose the action words that can help your resume become a strong one:

administered	introduced
advised	invented
analyzed	maintained
arranged	managed
assembled	met with
assumed responsibility	motivated
billed	negotiated
built	operated
carried out	orchestrated
channeled	ordered
collected	organized
communicated	oversaw
compiled	performed
completed	planned
conducted	prepared
contacted	presented
contracted	produced
coordinated	programmed
counseled	published
created	purchased
cut	recommended
designed	recorded
determined	reduced
developed	referred
directed	represented
dispatched	researched
distributed	reviewed
documented	saved
edited	screened
established	served as
expanded	served on
functioned as	sold
gathered	suggested
handled	supervised
hired	taught
implemented	tested
improved	trained
inspected	typed
interviewed	wrote

Now take a look at the information you put down on the work experience worksheets. Take that information and rewrite it in paragraph form, using verbs to highlight your actions and accomplishments. Let's look at an example, remembering that what matters here is the writing style, and not the particular job responsibilities given in our sample.

WORK EXPERIENCE
Regional Sales Manager

Manager of sales representatives from seven states. Responsible for twelve food chain accounts in the East. In charge of directing the sales force in planned selling toward specific goals. Supervisor and trainer of new sales representatives. Consulting for customers in the areas of inventory management and quality control.

Special Projects: Coordinator and sponsor of annual food industry sales seminar.

Accomplishments: Monthly regional volume went up 25 percent during my tenure while, at the same time, a proper sales/cost ratio was maintained. Customer/company relations improved significantly.

Below is the rewritten version of this information, using action words. Notice how much stronger it sounds.

WORK EXPERIENCE
Regional Sales Manager

Managed sales representatives from seven states. Handled twelve food chain accounts in the eastern United States. Directed the sales force in planned selling towards specific goals. Supervised and trained new sales representatives. Consulted for customers in the areas of inventory management and quality control. Coordinated and sponsored the annual Food Industry Seminar. Increased monthly regional volume 25 percent and helped to improve customer/company relations during my tenure.

Another way of constructing the work experience section is by using actual job descriptions. Job descriptions are rarely written using the proper resume language, but they do include all the information necessary to create this section of your resume. Take the description of one of the jobs your are including on your resume (if you have access to it), and turn it into an action-oriented paragraph. Below is an example of a job description followed by a version of the same description written using action words. Again, pay attention to the style of writing, as the details of your own work experience will be unique.

PUBLIC ADMINISTRATOR I

Responsibilities: Coordinate and direct public services to meet the needs of the nation, state, or community. Analyze problems; work with special committees and public agencies; recommend solutions to governing bodies.

Aptitudes and Skills: Ability to relate to and communicate with people; solve complex problems through analysis; plan, organize, and implement policies and programs. Knowledge of political systems; financial management; personnel administration; program evaluation; organizational theory.

WORK EXPERIENCE
Public Administrator I

Wrote pamphlets and conducted discussion groups to inform citizens of legislative processes and consumer issues. Organized and supervised 25 interviewers. Trained interviewers in effective communication skills.

Now that you have learned how to word your resume, you are ready for the next step in your quest for a winning resume: assembly and layout.

Chapter Three

ASSEMBLY AND LAYOUT

*A*t this point, you've gathered all the necessary information for your resume, and you've rewritten it using the language necessary to impress potential employers. Your next step is to assemble these elements in a logical order and then to lay them out on the page neatly and attractively in order to achieve the desired effect: getting that interview.

Assembly

The order of the elements in a resume makes a difference in its overall effect. Obviously, you would not want to put your name and address in the middle of the resume or your special skills section at the top. You want to put the elements in an order that stresses your most important achievements, not the less pertinent information. For example, if you recently graduated from school and have no full-time work experience, you will want to list your education before you list any part-time jobs you may have held during school. On the other hand, if you have been gainfully employed for several years and currently hold an important position in your company, you will want to list your work experience ahead of your education, which has become less pertinent with time.

There are some elements that are always included in your resume and some that are optional. Following is a list of essential and optional elements:

Essential	*Optional*
Name	Job Objective
Address	Honors
Phone Number	Special Skills
Work Experience	Professional Memberships
Education	Activities
References Phrase	Certificates and Licenses
	Personal Information

Your choice of optional sections depends on your own background and employment needs. Always use information that will put you and your abilities in a favorable light. If your honors are impressive, then be sure to include them in your resume. If your activities in school demonstrate particular talents necessary for the job you are seeking, then allow space for a section on activities. Each resume is unique, just as each person is unique.

Types of Resumes

So far, our discussion about resumes has involved the most common type—the *reverse chronological* resume, in which your most recent job is listed first and so on. This is the type of resume usually preferred by human resources directors, and it is the one most frequently used. However, in some cases this style of presentation is not the most effective way to highlight your skills and accomplishments.

For someone reentering the work force after many years or someone looking to change career fields, the *functional resume* may work best. This type of resume focuses more on achievement and less on the sequence of your work history. In the functional resume, your experience is presented by what you have accomplished and the skills you have developed in your past work.

A functional resume can be assembled from the same information you collected for your chronological resume. The main difference lies in how you organize this information. Essentially, the work experience section becomes two sections, with your job duties and accomplishments comprising one section and your employer's name, city, state, your position, and the dates employed making up another section. The first section is placed near the top of the resume, just below the job objective section, and can be called *Accomplishments* or *Achievements*. The second section, containing the bare essentials of your employment history, should come after the accomplishments section and can be titled *Work Experience* or *Employment History*. The other sections of your resume remain the same. The work experience section is the only one affected in the functional resume. By placing the section that focuses on your achievements first, you thereby draw attention to these achievements. This puts less emphasis on who you worked for and more emphasis on what you did and what you are capable of doing.

For someone changing careers, emphasis on skills and achievements is essential. The identities of previous employers, which may be unrelated to one's new job field, need to be downplayed. The functional resume accomplishes this task. For someone reentering the work force after many years, a functional resume is the obvious choice. If you lack full-time work experience, you will need to draw attention away from this fact and instead focus on your skills and abilities gained possibly through volunteer activities or part-time work. Education may also play a more important role in this resume.

Which type of resume is right for you will depend on your own personal circumstances. It may be helpful to create a chronological *and* a functional resume and then compare the two to find out which is more suitable. The sample resumes found in this book include both chronological and functional resumes. Use these resumes as guides to help you decide on the content and appearance of your own resume.

Layout

Once you have decided which elements to include in your resume and you have arranged them in an order that makes sense and emphasizes your achievements and abilities, then it is time to work on the physical layout of your resume.

There is no single appropriate layout that applies to every resume, but there are a few basic rules to follow in putting your resume on paper:

1. Leave a comfortable margin on the sides, top, and bottom of the page (usually 1 to 1½ inches).

2. Use appropriate spacing between the sections (usually 2 to 3 line spaces are adequate).

3. Be consistent in the *type* of headings you use for the different sections of your resume. For example, if you capitalize the heading EMPLOYMENT HISTORY, don't use initial capitals and underlining for a heading of equal importance, such as Education.

4. Always try to fit your resume onto one page. If you are having trouble fitting all your information onto one page, perhaps you are trying to say too much. Try to edit out any repetitive or unnecessary information or possibly shorten descriptions of earlier jobs. Be ruthless. Maybe you've included too many optional sections.

CHRONOLOGICAL RESUME

JUAN C. GARCIA
2103 AFTON STREET
TEMPLE HILL, MARYLAND 20748
HOME (301) 555-2419

EDUCATION:

Columbia University, New York, NY
Majors: Communications, Business
Degree expected: Bachelor of Science, 1990
Grade point average: 3.0
Regents Scholarship recipient
Columbia University Scholarship recipient

EXPERIENCE:

7/89-9/89

Graduate Business Library, Columbia University, NY
General library duties. Entered new students and
books onto computer files. Gave out microfiche.
Reserved and distributed materials.

9/88-5/89

German Department, Columbia Univeristy, NY
Performed general office duties. Offered extensive
information assistance by phone and in person.
Collated and proofread class materials. Assisted
professors in the gathering of class materials.

6/88-9/88

Loan Collections Department, Columbia University, NY
Initiated new filing system for the office. Checked
arrears in Bursar's Office during registration period.

9/87-5/88

School of Continuing Education, Columbia University, NY
Involved in heavy public contact as well as general
clerical duties.

SPECIAL ABILITIES:

Total fluency in Spanish. Currently studying German.
Can program in BASIC. Excellent research skills.

REFERENCES:

Available on request

FUNCTIONAL RESUME

CAROL BAKER
4420 Sunset Blvd.
Hollywood, CA 90027
213/555-9098

JOB SOUGHT: Promotion Director for a TV station.

SKILLS AND ACHEIVEMENTS

Promotion/Marketing

*Wrote and designed promotional pieces
*Evaluated content and direction of promotions
*Handled market research/demographic research
*Consulted clients on marketing plans

Video Production

*Handled shooting procedures, audio, lighting, casting and editing.
*Wrote and edited shooting scripts
*Determined production values for marketing accounts
*Oversaw postproduction and placement
*Coordinated presentations to clients

Media Planning

*Advised clients on media strategies
*Oversaw media budgets
*Determined and implemented marketing objectives
*Negotiated spot rates for clients

EMPLOYMENT HISTORY

Geary Advertising, Inc., Los Angeles, CA
Media Planner, 1984 - 1990

Goebert & Radner, Inc , Chicago, IL
Assistant Media Buyer, 1981 - 1984

Sears, Inc., Chicago, IL
Advertising Assistant, 1980 - 1981

EDUCATION

Drake University, Des Moines, IA
B.A. in Economics, 1980
Minor in Advertising
Phi Beta Kappa
Dean's List

References available on request

Don't let the idea of having to tell every detail about your life get in the way of producing a resume that is simple and straightforward. The more compact your resume, the easier it will be to read and the better an impression it will make for you.

In some cases, the resume will not fit on a single page, even after extensive editing. In such cases, the resume should be printed on two pages so as not to compromise clarity or appearance. Each page of a two-page resume should be marked clearly with your name and the page number, e.g., "Judith Ramirez, page 1 of 2." The pages should then be stapled together.

Try experimenting with various layouts until you find one that looks good to you. Always show your final layout to other people and ask them what they like or dislike about it, and what impresses them most about your resume. Make sure that is what you want most to emphasize. If it isn't, you may want to consider making changes in your layout until the necessary information is emphasized. Use the sample resumes in this book to get some ideas for laying out your resume.

Putting Your Resume in Print

Your resume should be typed or printed on good quality 8½″ × 11″ bond paper. You want to make as good an impression as possible with your resume; therefore, quality paper is a necessity. If you have access to a word processor with a good printer, or know of someone who does, make use of it. Typewritten resumes should only be used when there are no other options available.

After you have produced a clean original, you will want to make duplicate copies of it. Usually a copy shop is your best bet for producing copies without smudges or streaks. Make sure you have the copy shop use quality bond paper for all copies of your resume. Ask for a sample copy before they run your entire order. After copies are made, check each copy for cleanliness and clarity.

Another more costly option is to have your resume typeset and printed by a printer. This will provide the most attractive resume of all. If you anticipate needing a lot of copies of your resume, the cost of having it typeset may be justified.

Proofreading

After you have finished typing the master copy of your resume and before you go to have it copied or printed, you must thoroughly check it for typing and spelling errors. Have several people read it over just in case you may have missed an error. Misspelled words and typing mistakes will not make a good impression on a prospective employer, as they are a bad reflection on your writing ability and your attention to detail. With thorough and conscientious proofreading, these mistakes can be avoided.

The following are some rules of capitalization and punctuation that may come in handy when proofreading your resume:

Rules of Capitalization

- Capitalize proper nouns, such as names of schools, colleges, and universities, names of companies, and brand names of products.

- Capitalize major words in the names and titles of books, tests, and articles that appear in the body of your resume.

- Capitalize words in major section headings of your resume.

- Do not capitalize words just because they seem important.

- When in doubt, consult a manual of style such as *Words Into Type* (Prentice-Hall), or *The Chicago Manual of Style* (The University of Chicago Press). Your local library can help you locate these and other reference books.

Rules of Punctuation

- Use a comma to separate words in a series.

- Use a semicolon to separate series of words that already include commas within the series.

- Use a semicolon to separate independent clauses that are not joined by a conjunction.

- Use a period to end a sentence.

- Use a colon to show that the examples or details that follow expand or amplify the preceding phrase.

- Avoid the use of dashes.

- Avoid the use of brackets.

- If you use any punctuation in an unusual way in your resume, be consistent in its use.

- Whenever you are uncertain, consult a style manual.

Chapter Four

THE COVER LETTER

*O*nce your resume has been assembled, laid out, and printed to your satisfaction, the next and final step before distribution is to write your cover letter. Though there may be instances where you deliver your resume in person, most often you will be sending it through the mail. Resumes sent through the mail always need an accompanying letter that briefly introduces you and your resume. The purpose of the cover letter is to get a potential employer to read your resume, just as the purpose of your resume is to get that same potential employer to call you for an interview.

Like your resume, your cover letter should be clean, neat, and direct. A cover letter usually includes the following information:

1. Your name and address.

2. The date.

3. The name and address of the person and company to whom you are sending your resume.

4. The salutation ("Dear Mr." or "Dear Ms." followed by the person's last name, or "To Whom It May Concern").

5. An opening paragraph explaining why you are writing (in response to an ad, the result of a previous meeting, at the suggestion of someone you both know) and indicating your interest in the job being offered.

6. One or two more paragraphs that tell why you want to work for the company and what qualifications and experience you can bring to that company.

7. A final paragraph that closes the letter and requests that you be contacted for an interview. You may mention here that your references are available upon request.

8. The closing ("Sincerely," or "Yours Truly," followed by your signature with your name typed under it).

Your cover letter, including all of the information above, should be no more than one page in length. The language used should be polite, businesslike, and to the point. Do not attempt to tell your life story in the cover letter. A long and cluttered letter will only serve to put off the reader. Remember, you only need to mention a few of your accomplishments and skills in the cover letter. The rest of your information is in your resume. Each and every achievement should not be mentioned twice. If your cover letter is a success, your resume will be read and all pertinent information reviewed by your prospective employer.

Producing the Cover Letter

Cover letters should always be typed individually, since they are always written to particular individuals and companies. Never use a form letter for your cover letter. Each one should be as personal as possible. Of course, once you have written and rewritten your first cover letter to the point where you are satisfied with it, you certainly can use similar wording in subsequent letters.

After you have typed your cover letter on quality bond paper, be sure to proofread it as thoroughly as you did your resume. Again, spelling errors are a sure sign of carelessness, and you don't want that to be a part of your first impression on a prospective employer. Make sure to handle the letter and resume carefully to avoid any smudges, and then mail both your cover letter and resume in an appropriate sized envelope. Be sure to keep an accurate record of all the resumes you send out and the results of each mailing.

Numerous sample cover letters appear at the end of the book. Use them as models for your own cover letter or to get an idea of how cover letters are put together. Remember, every one is unique and depends on the particular circumstances of the individual writing it and the job for which he or she is applying.

About a week after mailing resumes and cover letters to potential employers, you will want to contact them by telephone. Confirm that your resume arrived, and ask whether an interview might be possible. Getting your foot in the door during this call is half the battle of a job search, and a strong resume and cover letter will help you immeasurably.

Chapter Five

SAMPLE RESUMES

This chapter contains dozens of sample resumes for people pursuing a wide variety of jobs and careers within this field.

There are many different styles of resumes in terms of graphic layout and presentation of information. These samples also represent people with varying amounts of education and work experience. Use these samples to model your own resume after. Choose one resume, or borrow elements from several different resumes to help you construct your own.

ROSEMARY DEBORAH PARKER

5509 E. George St. #442
Columbia, SC 29263
803/555-2893

CAREER OBJECTIVE: Magazine editor.

SKILLS & ACCOMPLISHMENTS:

* Evaluated submitted manuscripts for a monthly magazine.
* Handled copy editing and rewriting of manuscripts.
* Worked with artists and designers on layout aspects.
* Supervised the publication of an anthology of poetry.
* Served as proofreader for feature articles.
* Handled copy editing duties for local newspaper.
* Reported on events of local interest.
* Represented employer at several publishing conferences.

EMPLOYMENT HISTORY:

Carolina Woman, Columbia, SC
Assistant Editor, 1984 - present

Raleigh Gazette, Raleigh, NC
Copy editor/reporter, 1981 - 1983

EDUCATION:

Columbia University, Columbia, SC
B.A. in Journalism, 1981
Minor in English

HONORS:

Summa Cum Laude
Journalism Award, 1980
Henry Moffatt Scholarship recipient, 1978 - 1981

MEMBERSHIPS:

Southern Writers Association
American Association Of Magazine Publishers

References provided upon request

TERRI BAKKEMO

700 Thornborough Rd.
Chattanooga, TN 75221
615/555-2111

CAREER OBJECTIVE

A career in the field of broadcast journalism where I can utilize my experience in writing, editing and research.

EDUCATION

HOWARD UNIVERSITY, Washington, D.C.
Bachelor of Arts, Journalism, 1990

WORK EXPERIENCE

WDC-TV, Washington, D.C.
Research Assistant/News Department, Summer 1990
Assisted in the production of a news show. Served as a copy aide. Worked at UPI office during congressional hearings. Handled general research duties.

CAPITOL MAGAZINE, Washington, D.C.
Editorial Assistant to Senior Editor, Summer 1989
Coordinated an organized system of manuscript flow between editors. Assisted in editing and proofreading copy. Rewrote news articles and planned new stories and layout ideas.

CHATTANOOGA NEWS, Chattanooga, TN
Intern, Summer 1988
Assisted in layout, editing and reporting for local newspaper. Wrote and edited articles.

PARK ADVERTISING, INC., Chattanooga, TN
Creative Department Intern, Summer 1987
Handled proofreading and editing of copy. Assisted in demographic research.

HONORS

Rebook Scholarship, 1989, 1990
Dean's List

REFERENCES

Available on request

terri franks
15 nob hill
san francisco, ca   91405

job objective

graphic designer

work experience

terri franks design, san francisco, ca
freelance designer, 1986 to present
designed brochures, ads, posters. coordinated fashion shows.
created business systems.

berkeley college of design, berkeley, ca
graphic design intern, 1989
designed printed materials for university clients, including alumni journal
and admissions brochure.

fern labs, inc., palo alto, ca
graphics assistant, 1985 - 1986
designed and produced illustrations for brochures.

university of minnesota, minneapolis, mn
photographer, 1977 - 1979
took photos for university publications.

education

berkeley college of design, berkeley, ca
b.a. in graphic design, 1990
areas of concentration: photography, publication design, copywriting,
typography, packaging

university of minnesota, minneapolis, mn
b.a. in history, 1979

awards

northern california photography exihibit, 3rd place, 1989
berkeley student design show, honorable mention, 1989

references available upon request

MICHAEL ERVIN McDONALD
333 E. Rhett Drive
Augusta, GA 33390   404/555-0393

OBJECTIVE: Program director of a major market urban radio station.

WORK EXPERIENCE:

WGAU Radio, Augusta, GA
Producer/Announcer, 1988 - present
Produced weekly jazz music show for a non-commercial radio station.
Determined playlist and weekly adds for show. Placed special emphasis
on African-American artists and their work. Developed special feature
segments. Served as show's host.

WROB Radio, Robinson, IL
Program Director/Music Director, 1986 - 1988
Coordinated and presented the complete daily program schedule for a
non-commercial radio station which emphasized jazz music and public
affairs. Arranged work schedule for staff. Conducted planning meetings.
Made production assignments. Selected music to fit station's format with
the goal of increasing listenership.

Top Street Records, East St. Louis, IL
Sales Clerk, 1980 - 1985
Handled inventory and sales for jazz department. Ordered records based
on weekly sales reports. Conducted music research for two local radio
stations. Instituted marketing plan for department which resulted in
a 25% increase in sales quarterly.

WREE Radio, East St. Louis, IL
Producer/Announcer, 1977 - 1982
Produced two weekend jazz shows for non-commercial radio station. Served
as announcer for both shows. Interviewed contemporary jazz artists.
Researched and selected music for other jazz shows at the station.

EDUCATION:

Midwest School of Broadcasting, St. Louis, MO
Certificate, 1976

East St. Louis High School, East St. Louis, MO
Diploma, 1974

REFERENCES:

Available on request

GLORIA GARLAND

1220 Market St. #3   415/555-5508
San Francisco, CA   922990   415/555-5200

OBJECTIVE: A management level position in the publishing
                      industry.

**WORK
EXPERIENCE:**

                      BAY MAGAZINE, San Francisco, CA
                      Regional Manager, 1987 - present
                      Oversaw administration, negotiation and
                      maintenance of exchange agreements and sales
                      promotion. Tracked market changes, with
                      responsibility for executing responses to
                      developments. Led magazine's Eastern edition
                      through a reorganization period. Planned and
                      implemented new editions in the South.

                      SANDLER IMPORTS, Sausalito, CA
                      Sales Coordinator, 1983 - 1987
                      Managed ten field representatives. Handled
                      information dissemination and distribution. Co-
                      designed a full-color catalog. Placed advertising
                      in major trade publications. Promoted products at
                      trade shows. Maintained inventory status reports
                      and personnel records.

                      REDWOOD PUBLISHING CO., San Francisco, CA
                      Distribution Assistant, 1978 - 1983
                      Developed new distribution outlets through cold-
                      calls and follow-up visits. Increased
                      distribution in my district by 45% over a three-
                      year period. Coordinated a direct mail program
                      that increased magazine subscriptions 120%.

                      XEROX CO., Atlanta, GA
                      Sales representative, 1975 -1978
                      Sold and serviced office copiers to businesses and
                      schools in the greater Atlanta area. Maintained
                      good customer relations through frequent calls and
                      visits. Identified potential customers.

EDUCATION:

                      Miami University, Miami, OH
                      B.S. in Communications, 1974

GLORIA GARLAND - Page 2

PROFESSIONAL
MEMBERSHIPS:

American Publishing Association
National Association of Importers
Sausalito Community Association
San Francisco Chamber of Commerce

SEMINARS:

"Publishing in the 90's," Chicago, IL
"International Publishing," New York, NY

REFERENCES:

Available on request.

PETER KLEPT
PHOTOGRAPHY
GRAPHIC DESIGN

Address
554 Grambling Road
Santa Barbara, CA   97770
Phone: 815/555-2332

PROFESSIONAL EXPERIENCE

Photography

--Served as official photographer for the Nevada State Fair.
--Headed a team of photographers.
--Photographed products, promotions, press releases and publications.
--Worked with 35mm and 2 1/4 X 2 1/4 inch cameras, black and white, color and quick-processing methods.
--Landed UPI and AP releases.
--Experienced in photo developing.

Graphic Design

--Designed publication layouts and covers.
--Worked with paste-up and camera ready art.
--Produced brochures and folders.
--Created advertising layouts.
--Gained experience using a stat camera.

EMPLOYMENT HISTORY

Klept Photography, Santa Barbara, CA
Freelance Photographer, 1980 - present

California Design, Los Angeles, CA
Graphic Designer, 1984 -1987

Corlis Advertising, Topeka, KS
Staff Artist, 1982

University of Washington, Tacoma, WA
Photography Lab Assistant, 1978 - 1979

EDUCATION

University of Washington, Tacoma, WA
B.A. in Graphic Arts/Minor in Photography, 1979

Auber Junior College, Topeka, KS
Attended 1976 - 1977

References and portfolio available on request

James Thornborough Newton

1171 Davis St. #2
Evanston, IL 60202
708/555-2741

Objective: Staff Writer/Researcher for a news department of a newspaper where I can use my editorial, writing and reporting skills.

Education:

NORTHWESTERN UNIVERSITY, Evanston, IL
B.A. in Journalism & Political Science (Double Major)
Summa Cum Laude, June 1990

Accomplishments:

--Wrote regular column on political issues for campus newspaper.

--Won journalism award for feature series on "The Nuclear Threat."

--Interviewed people in the news.

--Covered local news events.

--Researched and wrote pamphlets for city council on crime, pollution, gentrification and zoning.

--Edited grant proposals for local theatre company.

--Served as assistant researcher for NBC opinion poll.

Employment History:

THE DAILY NORTHWESTERN, Evanston, IL
STAFF WRITER, 1988 - 1990

EVANSTON CITY COUNCIL, Evanston, IL
RESEARCHER/WRITER, 1989 - 1990

VICTORY GARDENS THEATER, Chicago, IL
EDITOR, 1988

NBC-TV, Chicago, IL
RESEARCHER, 1988

References:

Available on request

TERESA MORBITO
15 Fourth St. East
Boston, MA 02115
602/555-4009

JOB OBJECTIVE: Graphic Designer.

EXPERIENCE: New England News, Cambridge, MA
Manager, Advertising Dept., 1988 - 1990
Conceived and designed ads for publication.
Oversaw development, layout and typesetting.
Maintained financial records and accounts. Handled
staff hiring. Used stat camera and computer graphics.

Childs Advertising, Inc., Chicago, IL
Staff Artist, Summer 1987 - 1988
Involved in concept development, typesetting, design
and layout. Gained experience in halftone photography,
platemaking, stripping and finishing.

The Ledger, Chicago, IL
Cartoonist, 1987 - 1988
Drew cartoons for University of Chicago student
newspaper.

EDUCATION: Cambridge School of Design, Cambridge, MA
M.A. in Graphic Design, 1990
Areas of study included advertising, design, copywriting,
drawing, kinegraphics.

University of Chicago, Chicago, IL
B.A. in Visual Communications, 1988

SEMINARS: Eastern Design Conference, 1988, 1989
Illustrators Seminar, Boston, MA, 1988
Henry F. Droz Airbrush Workshop, Chicago, IL, 1987
Chicago Design Conference, 1987

MEMBERSHIPS: Cambridge Design Association, 1988 - present
Women in Film, Chicago, IL, 1986 - 1988
Progressive Design Club, New York, NY 1985 - present

REFERENCES: Available upon request

GERALD SCHWARTZ
10 Downing St. #230
Detroit, MI   53309
313/555-0009

JOB OBJECTIVE

An entry-level position in a multimedia production company.

ACCOMPLISHMENTS

Graphic Design

--Created concepts and layouts.
--Completed mechanicals for brochures, posters and books.
--Managed production department of a publishing company.
--Oversaw typography, stripping, printing and binding.
--Operated a stat camera.

Audio Visual

--Shot still photographs for a pictorial essay.
--Served as freelance photographer for various publications.
--Handled portrait work and advertising photography.
--Completed training in computer graphics, multi-image
graphics and multi-image programming.

Writing

--Edited course catalogs for a university.
--Contributed articles to campus newspaper.
--Reviewed manuscripts for a publisher.

WORK HISTORY

HELICON PUBLISHING, INC., Detroit, MI
PRODUCTION MANAGER, 1987 - present

FREELANCE GRAPHIC DESIGNER/PHOTOGRAPHER, Detroit, MI
1983 - present

DELBERT ADVERTISING, INC., Saginaw, MI
GRAPHIC DESIGNER, 1983 - 1984

EDUCATION

DETROIT SCHOOL OF DESIGN, Detroit, MI
Compugraphics, Photography, 1986

SAGINAW COLLEGE, Saginaw, MI
B.A. in Art, 1982

REFERENCES AVAILABLE UPON REQUEST

HARRISON CRUMPET
3338 W. Redbook Drive
Amarillo, TX 78077
806/555-1910

JOB SOUGHT: Director of Traffic for a television station.

WORK EXPERIENCE:

WARM-TV, Amarillo, TX

Assistant Director of Traffic, 1987 - present

Acted as contact between syndication companies and station.
Created TV log. Established sales availabilities. Screened and
processed tapes and films. Pulled and disemminated teletype
information.

WPIX-TV, El Paso, TX

Assistant to the Traffic Director, 1985 - 1987

Handled maintenance of traffic boards. Filed and updated TV logs.
Prepared advanced program information for TV listings. Ordered
films and tapes for future use. Organized processing procedure for
PSA's.

Assistant to Head Programmer, 1984 - 1985

Oversaw program scheduling. Updated and maintained TV log.
Handled public service spots. Routed correspondence for Head
Programmer.

EDUCATION:

Amarillo State College, Amarillo, TX
B.A. in Communications, 1983
Area of concentration - Television

Horton Junior College, Horton, TX
1980 - 1981

MEMBERSHIPS:

Texas Communications Association
Amarillo Citizens Council

References available on request

GEOFFREY HODGES
329 Kedzie Ave. #2
Evanston, IL 60202
708/555-4727

WRITING EXPERIENCE

Arco Publishing Group, Chicago, IL
Book Writer, 1988 - present
Author of Environmental Impact and Home Improvements.

National College of Education, Evanston, IL
Editor, Grants Department, 1988
Edited grant proposals. Created brochure on grant programs.

Stagebill Magazine, New York, NY
Feature Writer, 1987 - 1988

Rapport Theater, Chicago, IL
Editor/Research Assistant, 1985 - 1987
Researched, compiled and edited study guides for seven productions.

WORK EXPERIENCE

Northwestern University, Evanston, IL
Administrative Assistant, 1987 -1989
Drafted and edited correspondence. Managed expense accounts. Handled scheduling of appointments and preparation of course materials.

Rapport Theater, Chicago, IL
Office Manager, 1985 -1987
Maintained payroll and financial records. Interviewed, selected and supervised work-study students. Organized and monitored registration for Theater Center classes.

EDUCATION

Northwestern University, Evanston, IL
Bachelor of Arts with Honors in English, 1984
Cumulative GPA: 3.76/4.00

HONORS

Phi Beta Kappa, 1984
Honors in English, 1984
Dean's List, Seven Quarters
Mayo Writing Prize, Honorable Mention, 1982
Valedictorian, 1980

REFERENCES

Available on request

ELIZABETH PERLMAN
Sandler Hall
144 Glendon Ave.
Room 225
Los Angeles, CA 90289
213/555-2384

EDUCATION

UCLA, Los Angeles, CA
Bachelor of Arts in Broadcast Production
Expected June 1991

HONORS

Phi Beta Kappa
Dean's List four semesters
Peter J. Tolbrook Award, 1989

ACTIVITIES

President, Student Government
Freshman Advisor
Homecoming Planning Committee
Volleyball Team

WORK EXPERIENCE

NBC, Inc., Burbank, CA
Sales Intern, 1990
Assisted sales staff in the areas of research,
demographics, sales forecasts, identifying new
customers and promotion.

UCLA, Los Angeles, CA
Research/Office Assistant, 1988-89
Researched and compiled materials for department
professors. Arranged filing system and supervisor's
library. Organized department inventory.

SPECIAL SKILLS

Fluent in Spanish. Experience using WORDSTAR and dBASE
III software programs.

References available on request

TERRY SANDY

1440 Graper Drive
Salt Lake City, UT   83389
801/555-3332

OBJECTIVE: Music Director of a radio station.

EXPERIENCE: KBGG-RADIO, Salt Lake City, UT
              MUSIC DIRECTOR, 1984 - present
              Oversaw weekly selection of music. Served as
              liaison to record labels, music venues and
              artists. Supervised music assistants. Conducted
              music tests with the general public.

              KOOP-RADIO, Las Vegas, NV
              ASSISTANT MUSIC DIRECTOR, 1980 - 1984
              Assisted program director with music selection and
              programming. Cultivated new record label and
              venue contacts.

              POP PRODUCTIONS, Los Angeles, CA
              PRODUCER, 1978 - 1980
              Produced various commercials for radio.

              WWWW-RADIO, St. Louis, MO
              PRODUCER/ANNOUNCER, 1970 - 1977
              Produced a Top 40 hit music show for radio.
              Served as announcer, as well as producer.
              Researched and selected music. Interviewed
              artists.

EDUCATION: WASHINGTON UNIVERSITY, St. Louis, MO
              M.A. in Broadcasting, 1968
              B.A. in Communications, 1966

REFERENCES: Available on request.

GREG GOLD
1661 Corn Row Drive
Cedar Rapids, IA 53309
319/555-2909 (Home)
319/555-8888 (Work)

JOB OBJECTIVE: Engineering Technician/Cameraman

SKILLS:

* all camera operations for film and video

* studio lighting

* set design

* film editing

* dubbing

* gaffing

* audio-video switching

* mixing

* technical troubleshooting

EMPLOYMENT HISTORY:

WCED-TV, Cedar Rapids, IA
Engineering Assistant, 1987 - present

Drawbridge Productions, Des Moines, IA
Assistant Camerman, Summer 1986

WWOR Radio, Jackson, MS
Engineer, 1985 - 1987

EDUCATION:

Jackson University, Jackson, MS
B.A. in Communication Arts, 1987

REFERENCES:

Available on request.

REBECCA PORTER UPJOHN

100 West Tenth St.
Bloomington, IN 46703   317/555-3893

OBJECTIVE: A career in photography.

EDUCATION

INDIANA STATE UNIVERSITY, Bloomington, IN
Bachelor of Arts, Visual Communications, 1990
Emphasis in Photography. Coursework included:
Studio lighting/Bank lighting, Advertising/Product Photography,
Photojournalism, Portrait Photography, Advertising, Copywriting.

WORK EXPERIENCE

INDIANA STATE UNIVERSITY, Bloomington, IN
PHOTOGRAPHER, MEDIA CENTER, 1989 - 1990
Worked directly with designer to fulfill their photographic
needs. Used high speed film to photograph dramatic events in
existing light. Contributed photographs to university
publications. Mastered standard film processing E6.

FREELANCE PHOTOGRAPHER, 1988 - 1990
Handled advertising, publication, passport and portrait
photography.

INDIANA STATE UNIVERSITY, Bloomington, IN
STUDENT ASSISTANT, BLOOMINGTON LIBRARY, 1987 - 1988
Interfaced with the public. Used office computers and copiers.
Handled data entry.

EXHIBITS

Bloomington Library, 1990
Parker Gallery, 1989
Community Show, 1989
Campus Center, 1988

MEMBERSHIPS

Women in Photography
Designers in Progress
Communications Club
Advertising Club

WORKSHOPS

Indirect Lighting, 1990
Outdoor Photography, 1989
Color & Pigments, 1989

PORTFOLIO AND REFERENCES AVAILABLE

MARY ALICE MOORE
3230 W. Alsip Drive #3C
Milwaukee, WI   53100
419/555-8908

OBJECTIVE: Public relations assistant for a major U.S.
                  airline company.

EXPERIENCE: Midwest Airlines, Inc., Milwaukee, WI
                  Sales representative, 1988 - present
                  Sold reservations for domestic flights, hotels and
                  car rentals. Marketed travel packages through
                  travel agencies. Negotiated airline and hotel
                  discounts for customers. Devised itineraries and
                  solved customers' travel related problems.

                  Travel in the Main, Evanston, IL
                  Travel Agent, 1980 - 1988
                  Handled customer reservations for airlines,
                  hotels, and car rentals. Advised customers on
                  competitive travel packages and prices.
                  Interacted with all major airlines, hotel chains
                  and car rental companies.

EDUCATION: University of Wisconsin, Beloit, WI
                  B.A. in Anthropology, 1956

SPECIAL
SKILLS: Hands-on experience using most travel-related
                  computer systems, including Apollo.

                  Working knowledge of German, French and Polish.

REFERENCES: Available on request.

HARRIET SCHUMACHER

1414 N. Montebello Drive
Berkeley, CA   98028
415/555-4930

EDUCATION: University of California at Berkeley
                             Bachelor of Science in Journalism
                             Expected June 1991

HONORS: Beta Gamma Upsilon Honorary Society
                             Dean's list
                             Manley Writing Award, 1989

ACTIVITIES: Treasurer, Gamma Gamma Gamma Sorority
                             Freshman Advisor
                             Homecoming Planning Committee
                             Alumni Welcoming Committee

WORK
EXPERIENCE: New York Post, New York, NY
                             Intern, 1990
                             Assisted in layout, editing and reporting for
                             local newspaper. Wrote and edited articles.
                             Handled preparatory research for local sports
                             events.

                             University of California at Berkeley
                             Office Assistant, Journalism School, 1988-
                             1990
                             Assisted with registrations, filing and
                             typing. Arranged application materials.
                             Assembled course packs.

SPECIAL SKILLS: Fluent in German. Hands-on computer
                             experience using LOTUS 123 and dBASE III.

REFERENCES: Available on request.

GERMANIA REDSON
Freelance Writing--Editing--Research

666 Torn Leaf Rd.
Hagerstown, MD   03394   301/555-3921

FREELANCE EXPERIENCE

Writing/Editing

*Served as editor for a series of books on cooking.
*Collaborated on writing and editing projects for a public
 relations firm.
*Edited a book on international travel in Spanish and English.
*Wrote brochures for a health insurance company.
*Published articles in magazine and newspapers.

Research

*Researched and compiled bibliographies for several books.
*Interviewed musician and songwriters for background for a book
 on the music industry.
*Managed reference services at a university library.
*Conducted extensive research on the health insurance industry
 for brochures.

Book Evaluation

*Evaluated manuscripts and produced reader's reports for three
 publishers.
*Reviewed selected books for local publications.
*Wrote a monthly book review column for community newsletter.

EMPLOYMENT HISTORY

1982 - 1990   Freelance Writer/Editor, Hagerstown, MD

1978 - 1982   Librarian, University of Maryland
                Princess Ann, MD

1974 - 1982   Library Assistant, Hagerstown Public Library
                Hagerstown, MD

1966 - 1974   Sales Person, Poppy Books
                Watersford, CT

EDUCATION

UNIVERSITY OF MARYLAND, Princess Ann, MD
B.A. in History, 1961
Cum Laude, Minor in Creative Writing

References provided on request

WILLIAM HARRIS

P.O. Box 4112
Fargo, ND 52289
701/555-3930

OBJECTIVE

To obtain an entry level position at a commercial radio station.

RADIO EXPERIENCE

WND-RADIO, Fargo, ND
ASSISTANT GENERAL MANAGER, 1989 – 1990
Assisted in the management of a student-run college radio station. Helped to direct and supervise a board of directors and an on-air staff to insure efficient day-to-day operations. Established music format guidelines and made other management-oriented decisions. Wrote and edited budget proposals. Assisted in financial matters.

WND-RADIO, Fargo, ND
ALTERNATIVE MUSIC DIRECTOR, 1987 – 1990
Created and implemented station alternative music format. Managed, scheduled and trained a staff of 15 on-air disc jockeys. Planned and organized club performances by local bands in conjunction with the station. Served as on-air personality.

WORK EXPERIENCE

FOSTER'S CANTINA, Fargo, ND
Waiter, 1989

GANDY'S SHOES, Yucca, ND
Salesman, 1987 – 1988

EDUCATION

FARGO COLLEGE, Fargo, ND
B.S. in Business Administration, 1990

ACTIVITIES

Studio Engineer, 1987 – 1990
News Announcer, 1988
Treasurer, Glee Club, 1989 – 1990
Football Team, 1987 – 1988

REFERENCES

Provided on request

LISA STANSFIELD

14 E. ThreePenny Road
Detroit, MI   33290
313/555-3489

OBJECTIVE

A management position in public relations where I can utilize my promotion and marketing experience.

WORK EXPERIENCE

SEVEN ELEVEN INC., Detroit, MI
Marketing Director, 1986 - present
Developed a successful marketing campaign for a convenience store chain. Initiated and maintained a positive working relationship with radio and print media. Implemented marketing strategies to increase sales at less profitable outlets. Designed a training program for store managers and staff.

SUPER VACUUM CO., Bloomfield Hills, MI
Marketing Representative, 1982 -1986
Demonstrated vacuums in specialty and department stores. Reported customer reactions to manufacturers. Designed fliers and advertising to promote products. Made frequent calls to retail outlets.

REBO CARPETS, INC., Chicago, IL
Assistant to Sales Manager, 1977 - 1982
Handled both internal and external areas of sales and marketing, including samples, advertising and pricing. Served as company sales representative and sold carpeting to retail outlets.

EDUCATION

UNIVERSITY OF MICHIGAN, Ann Arbor, MI
B.A. Marketing, 1976

SEMINARS

Michigan Marketing Workshop, 1988, 1989
Sales and Marketing Association Seminars, 1984

References available on request.

JONNI KARBERST
144 Woodbine
#445
Albuquerque, NM
88299
505/555-4909

CAREER OBJECTIVE

Graphic Design

EMPLOYMENT HISTORY

Fox Graphics, Albuquerque, NM
Graphic Designer, 1989 - present
Oversaw accounts from concept through production. Logged
expenses. Approved layout. Contracted freelance artists.
Operated computerized typesetting equipment.

Arizona Register, Phoenix, AZ
Production Manager, 1988 - 1989
Supervised staff of five designers. Coordinated typesetting
and camera schedules. Consistently met deadlines.
Coordinated advertising for daily and Sunday editions.
Maintained supply stock.

Staff Designer, 1987 - 1988
Designed and produced editorial and advertising layouts.
Developed and implemented ad strategies. Created
promotional materials.

Mink Design, Phoenix, AZ/Albuquerque, NM
Freelance Designer, 1987- present
Produced posters, logos, brochures and ads for a variety of
companies and organizations.

EDUCATION

Albuquerque School of Design, Albuquerque, NM
Studied Advanced Compugraphics, Summer, 1990

University of Arizona, Phoenix, AZ
Bachelor of Arts in Design, 1986
Design Honor Award
Photography Honor Award

University of Nevada, Carson City, NV
Studied liberal arts, 1983 - 1984

References available upon request

JANIS DARIEN

345 W. 3rd St.   Telephone: 617/555-3291
#42
Boston, MA   02210

JOB OBJECTIVE: A career in the field of advertising.

EDUCATION: Boston University, Boston, MA

                    B.A. in Advertising, 1990
                    Dean's List four quarters
                    3.45 GPA in major field
                    3.21 GPA overall
                    Homecoming Planning Committee

                    Plan to pursue graduate studies towards a Master's degree
                    in Marketing at Boston University, Evening Division.

                    Central High School, Evansville, IN

                    Graduated 1986
                    Top 10% of class
                    Business manager and coordinator of student newspaper
                    Vice President of Senior class
                    Student Council
                    Pep Club

WORK EXPERIENCE: Lewis Advertising Agency, Boston, MA
                    Marketing Assistant, Summer 1989
                    Assisted Marketing Manager in areas of promotion, product
                    development and demographic analysis.

                    Paterno Marketing, Boston, MA
                    Telephone Interviewer, Summer 1987 & 1988

                    White Hen Pantry, Evansville, IN
                    Cashier, Summer 1986

SPECIAL SKILLS: Fluent in French. Familiar with various computer hardware and
                    software.

REFERENCES: Available on request

SAGU RUGAT
    881 S. Evers St.
        Trenton, NJ 08778
            609/555-4903

        OBJECTIVE

A career in graphic design.

        EXPERIENCE

Masters Advertising, Trenton, NJ
Graphic Designer, 1989-1990
Handled development of concepts. Consulted clients.
Prepared camera-ready art. Used stat camera.

Newark College, Newark, NJ
Graphic Designer, University Art Gallery, 1988-1989
Designed posters and brochures for art exhibitions.

Newark College, Newark, NJ
Art Director, University Publications, 1989
Compiled and edited visuals for publications.

Newark College, Newark, NJ
Graphic Designer, Media Center, 1987-1988
Oversaw concept development. Consulted clients on design
choices. Prepared camera-ready art. Used compugraphic
headliner and stat camera.

        EDUCATION

Newark College, Newark, NJ
B.A. in Visual Communications, 1990
Course of study: publication design, corporate identity,
lettering, photography, kinegraphics, compugraphics and
packaging.

        MEMBERSHIPS

ADAC, Newark, NJ
Progressive Designers, Trenton, NJ

        AWARDS

Newark College Art Show, Best in Show, 1989

References available upon request

PERRY WATKINS, JR.

5029 Castro St.
San Francisco, CA 99888
415/555-3800 (Day)
415/555-2213 (Evening)

WORK EXPERIENCE

HOUSEWISE MAGAZINE, San Francisco, CA
Director of Operations, 1985 - present
Supervised 30 regional managers and offices with 519 employees.
Oversaw all local operations, including circulation, advertising
sales, promotion/marketing and $22 million salary and budget
administration. Increased ad sales by $7 million, an 18%
increase over three years.

Assistant to Editorial Manager, 1978 - 1985
Coordinated all of magazine's configuration changes. Served as
operations liaison to Housewise International. Initiated
subscription sales programs and formulated marketing strategies.
Developed and implemented all edition modifications in order to
boost circulation and optimize advertising sales.

KEYBOARD MAGAZINE, Los Angeles, CA
Assistant Publisher, 1972 - 1978
Reduced magazine to standard size which resulted in a substantial
reduction in paper and production costs. Helped magazine to meet
the changing needs of readership and advertisers. Supervised an
office of eleven.

Advertising Manager, 1965 - 1972
Generated $300,000 in advertising revenues. Increased consumer
awareness of the magazine which led to increased sales -
circulation grew an average of 22% each year. Stabilized
downward trends in circulation.

TRENDS MAGAZINE, Miami, FL
Regional Manager, 1958 - 1965
Oversaw administration, negotiation and maintenance of exchange
agreements and sales promotion. Tracked market changes, with
responsibility for executing responses to developments. Led
magazine's Eastern edition through a reorganization period.
Planned and implemented new editions in the South.

PERRY WATKINS, JR. - 2

EDUCATION

<u>UNIVERSITY OF IOWA</u>, Dubuque, IA
M.A. in Journalism, 1957

<u>BARTON UNIVERSITY</u>, Akron, OH
B.A. in History, 1956

PROFESSIONAL MEMBERSHIPS

Entertainment Publishers Society
National Association of Magazine Publishers
Castro Neighborhood Improvement Committee

REFERENCES

Available on request

ROBERT MULLET

5500 Seal Test Rd.
Shreveport, LA   22909
318/555-3893

OBJECTIVE: A career in photography.

EDUCATION

SHREVEPORT COLLEGE, Shreveport, LA
Bachelor of Arts, Visual Communications, 1990
Emphasis in Photography. Coursework included:
Studio lighting/Bank lighting, Advertising/Product Photography,
Photojournalism, Portrait Photography, Advertising, Copywriting.

WORK EXPERIENCE

SHREVEPORT COLLEGE, Shreveport, LA
PHOTOGRAPHER, MEDIA CENTER, 1989 - 1990
Worked directly with designer to fulfill their photographic
needs. Used high speed film to photograph dramatic events in
existing light. Contributed photographs to university
publications. Mastered standard film processing E6.

FREELANCE PHOTOGRAPHER, 1988 - 1990
Handled advertising, publication, passport and portrait
photography.

SHREVEPORT COLLEGE, Shreveport, LA
STUDENT ASSISTANT, MING LIBRARY, 1987 - 1988
Interfaced with the public. Used office computers and copiers.
Handled data entry.

EXHIBITS

Ming Library, 1990
Regis Gallery, 1989
Community Show, 1989

MEMBERSHIPS

Designers in Progress
Communications Club
Advertising Club

WORKSHOPS

Avant Graphics, 1990
Outdoor Photography, 1989
Color & Pigments, 1989

PORTFOLIO AND REFERENCES AVAILABLE

CARLOS DIEGO
700 E. Park
Brooklyn, NY   12007
718/555-7223

JOB OBJECTIVE: Art Director for a large east coast advertising
agency.

WORK
EXPERIENCE:

Samuel Levinson Agency, New York, NY
Senior Art Director, 1982 - present
Staff Artist, 1980 - 1982
Oversaw all artwork. Held responsibility for hiring artists,
researchers, copywriters and creative assistants. Conferred with
clients regarding advertising strategy. Formulated design
concepts. Assigned work to artists, photographers and writers.

Diego, Inc., Philadelphia, PA
Freelance Commercial Artist, 1974 - 1980
Produced general boardwork, illustrations, layouts, mechanicals
for a department store chain and several ad agencies.

Sandler Corporation, Chicago, IL
Researcher/Copywriter, 1970 - 1974
Researched market for products. Conducted comparison studies
with other products. Devised concepts for ads. Wrote copy for
ads, flyers and inserts. Made sales presentations.

EDUCATION:

Harvard University, Boston, MA
B.A. in Advertising, 1973

Redwood School of Design, Providence, RI
Summer 1973

Art Institute of San Francisco, San Francisco, CA
Summer 1972

REFERENCES:

Available upon request

HERMAN FOLDE
FREELANCE PHOTOGRAPHER/DESIGNER
800 Himer Road
La Jolla, CA 94340
619/555-1132

PROFESSIONAL EXPERIENCE

Folde Photography, La Jolla, CA
Freelance Photographer, 1980 - present

Served as official photographer for the California State Fair.
Headed a team of photographers. Photographed products,
promotions, press releases and publications. Worked with 35mm
and 2 1/4 X 2 1/4 inch cameras, black and white, color and quick-
processing methods. Landed UPI and AP releases. Experienced in
photo developing.

Sun Design, Los Angeles, CA
Graphic Designer, 1984 -1987

Designed publication layouts and covers. Worked with paste-up
and camera ready art. Produced brochures and folders. Created
advertising layouts. Gained experience using a stat camera.

EDUCATION

University of New Mexico, Albuquerque, MN
B.A. in Graphic Arts/Minor in Photography, 1979

Teepe Junior College, Omaha, NE
Attended 1976 - 1977

SHOWS

San Diego Photo Exhibition, 1978 - 1990
La Jolla Community Fair, 1980 - 1990
Magazine Fair, 1985 - 1986

References and portfolio available on request

YOLANDA FINKELSTEIN
54444 S. MAGNOLIA
NORTH HOLLYWOOD, CA 90042
818/555-2909
818/555-2789

CAREER OBJECTIVE

Commercial artist for an advertising agency.

SKILLS AND ACCOMPLISHMENTS

*Produced line drawings for magazine ads, slides and promotional materials.

*Gained experience in watercolors and acrylics.

*Handled all aspects of production from layout to finished product.

*Designed boardwork, paste-ups and reproductions.

*Took photos for university publications.

EMPLOYMENT HISTORY

LA Style Magazine, Burbank, CA
Commercial Artist, Summers 1988 - present

University of California, Northridge, CA
Designer, University Publications, 1990

University of California, Northridge, CA
Photographer, Northridge News, 1988 - 1990

EDUCATION:

University of California, Northridge, CA
B.A. in Commercial Art, expected 1991

WORKSHOPS:

Illustration Workshop, Art Institute of Chicago, 1989
Pacific Design Seminar, Los Angeles, CA 1988

References available on request.

RANDALL C. CALDWELL

6500 Rivercomb Drive #422
Washington, DC   01990
202/555-4421

OBJECTIVE: A career in the advertising industry.

EDUCATION: Georgetown University, Washington, DC
                  B.A. in Advertising, 1987
                  Major Fields: Advertising, Marketing, Graphic
                  Arts, Journalism, Business

SKILLS AND ACCOMPLISHMENTS:

                  *Handled four accounts for advertising
                  agency.
                  *Assisted with traffic control.
                  *Served as intermediary between client and account
                  executives.
                  *Assisted in writing copy and designing ads for
                  magazine copy.
                  *Computed ad sizes.
                  *Translated data from dummy to production work-
                  sheets and distributed for review.
                  *Provided informational assistance to clients.
                  *Wrote feature articles on local community news,
                  including education, sports, politics and the
                  arts.
                  *Provided photos and illustrations in support of
                  various articles.

WORK
EXPERIENCE: Simon & Simon, Inc., Baltimore, MD
                  Advertising Intern, Summer 1986

                  Capitol Life Magazine, Washington, DC
                  Advertising Assistant, Part-Time, 1985

                  Washington News, New Brunswick, ME
                  Free-lance writer, 1984 - 1986

HONORS: Summa Cum Laude, 1987
                  Dean's List
                  Winterburg Scholarship, 1986

REFERENCES: Provided if requested.

GERALD ROBERT SCAMPI

4890 W. 57th St.
New York, NY 10019
212/555-3678

JOB OBJECTIVE

Vice President of promotion for a communications company.

PROFESSIONAL
EXPERIENCE

1983-1987   ATLANTIC RECORDS, New York, NY
Promotion Manager. Developed and executed all marketing
strategy for record promotion in New York, New Jersey and
Massachussetts. Interfaced with sales department and retail
stores to insure adequate product placement. Attended various
company sponsored sales, marketing and management seminars.

1973-1982   RSO RECORDS, Miami, FL
Promotion Manager. Planned all marketing strategy for record
promotions in the southeast U.S. Worked closely with sales and
touring bands to insure product visibility in the marketplace.

1971-1973   WCFL RADIO, Chicago, IL
Served as a morning DJ. Played CHR music. Made TV appearances
and public events appearances for the station. Organized and
staffed station's news department. Promoted to Music Director
after one year.

1966-1971   WGLT RADIO, Atlanta, GA
Served as Program Director, Music Director and News Director
during my tenure.

EDUCATION

COLUMBIA COLLEGE, Chicago, IL
Attended 1965 -1966
Studied Audio Engineering

References available on request

REGINA REGAN JOHNSON

702 Fern Dell
Glenview, IL 60067
708/555-4928

WRITING EXPERIENCE

Screenplays

Completed spec screenplay, CARNIVAL and treatments for
forthcoming spec screenplays: HAROLD AND FRED,
DREAMHOUSE, THE OUTSIDER, JOB-HUNTING, THE
ADVENTURES OF LITTLE LEON, and THE CARPET SWEEPER.

Children's Books

Wrote Hats (now in revision at Houghton Mifflin, Boston,
MA) and The Carpet Sweeper.

Short Stories

Wrote A Garden - collected short stories and two one-act
plays.

Published Writings

Published twice in The Christian Science Monitor on the
"Home Forum" and "Home and Family" pages. Published poems
and children's articles in The Christian Science
Sentinel.

PROFESSIONAL MEMBERSHIPS

Participating as a full member in:
   Women in Film, Chicago, IL
   Society of Children's Book Writers
   The Writers - Deerfield, IL
Associate member: Society of Midland Authors, Chicago, IL

EDUCATION

Northwestern University, Evanston, IL

Received BA in English, June, 1985.
Majored in Theatre and English for three years at
Northwestern University, then returned to Northwestern
after rearing two sons to complete BA degree in English.
Admitted, shortly thereafter, to the Writing Program.
Studied fiction writing under Jonathan Brent and Mary
Gray Hughes, and playwriting with David Rush. Recently,
completed a Graduate course in feature film writing with
Mary-Terese Cozzola at Northwestern University.

References available upon request

GEORGE T. BENSON

1800 W. Pico
Santa Monica, CA 90110
213/555-8938
213/555-8000

JOB OBJECTIVE

A public relations . position in the entertainment industry where I can
utilize my communication skills, contacts and industry background.

WORK EXPERIENCE

TBC MARKETING, Burbank, CA
Independent Marketing, 1988 - present
Coordinated stock with regional distributors. Generated exposure and interest
at local retail store and one-stops in conjuction with local and regional
airplay. Suggested supplemental marketing strategies based on airplay, sales
and percentage of penetration.

HITS MAGAZINE, Van Nuys, CA
National Marketing Coordinator, 1986 - 1988
Sold charts and tracking information to radio, artist management and record
labels. Handled tracking for all accounts on charting product. Interacted
with radio accounts weekly regarding early chart information.

CASHBOX MAGAZINE, Los Angeles, CA
Regional Sales Representative, 1983 - 1986
Managed and developed west coast territory for Cashbox Service Network.
Provided chart information, including bullet criteria, points, sales/airplay
ratios to independent marketing companies and management. Serviced retail
accounts and created new marketing strategies for product tracking services.

PARKER MANUFACTURING, Flint, MI
Sales Representative, 1979 - 1983
Negotiated and sold contract repairs on industrial equipment. Wrote daily
technical reports on product movement and inventory. Consistently met and
exceeded sales quotas for each quarter.

EDUCATION

MICHIGAN STATE UNIVERSITY, Grand Rapids, MI
B.A., Communications, 1979

REFERENCES

Available on request

SANDRA SWEENEY
1401 N. La Brea
Hollywood, CA 90028
213/555-1298

GOAL: Traffic Manager at an advertising agency or corporate
       advertising department.

**WORK
EXPERIENCE:**

MUSIC CONNECTION MAGAZINE, Burbank, CA
Assistant Production Manager, 1986 - present

Oversaw all aspects of production and printing at a national
publication. Involved in heavy client and agency contact.
Organized all art, mechanicals and final films with
stripping department. Handled in-depth media background
contact with other media. Produced copy for ads.

CIRCUIT CITY, Hollywood, CA
Assistant to Promotion Director, 1982 - 1986

Conducted all in-store promotions and events. Place
advertising and publicity in local publications. Consulted
on grand-opening of Santa Monica store. Assisted customers
frequently.

EDUCATION:

UNIVERSITY OF SOUTHERN CALIFORNIA, Los Angeles, CA
B.S. in Marketing, 1971

HONORS:

Cum Laude, 1971
Dean's List, 1970 - 1971
Henry Seaver Scholarship, 1969

References available upon request

WENDY WIMMER

45330 Santa Monica Blvd.
Los Angeles, CA 90088
213/555-8393 (Day)
213/555-3839 (Evening)

OBJECTIVE: Senior Copywriter for a publishing company.

EMPLOYMENT
EXPERIENCE: Winterpark Publishing, Inc., Pasadena, CA
Staff Copywriter, 1988 - present
Researched and wrote book proposals, including
sales letter, synopsis and sample chapters.
Created advertising copy for company's book
catalogs. Composed captions for illustrations and
side bars. Handled layout and paste-up. Edited
and rewrote manuscripts in preparation for
publication.

Wendy Wimmer, Inc., Los Angeles, CA
Free-lance Writer, 1984 - 1988
Edited five technical manuals on computer
software. Scripted four industrial films for
various food service companies. Developed two
book ideas and drafted sales proposals for a book-
packaging company. Wrote several articles that
were published in national magazines. Composed
copy for department store catalog.

EDUCATION: UCLA, Los Angeles, CA
B.A. in English, 1984

HONORS: Phi Beta Kappa, 1984
Dean's List, 1983, 1984
Robert D. Mayo Writing Competition,
  Second Prize, 1983
Writing Club, President, 1984

References available upon request

JEANNETTE HOBBS

8 E. Magnolia Court
Apartment 2
Dallas, TX   73389
206/555-1890

JOB OBJECTIVE

Assistant Director of Public Relations

EMPLOYMENT HISTORY

SIX FLAGS OVER DALLAS, Dallas, TX
Administrative Assistant to Director of Public Relations,
1986 - present

Prepared news releases. Maintained personal media contacts.
Prepared and edited copy for brochures, ads and posters. Helped
to develop advertising plans. Edited copy for newsletter.
Prepared and distributed newsletter to patrons. Handled all
booking for live entertainment.

Office Manager, 1983 - 1986

Coordinated workshops and seminars on publicity. Handled group
travel and hotel arrangements. Supervised an office staff of
eight. Maintained business calendar. Organized staff meetings.
Booked convention space. Prepared financial reports.

EDUCATION

BROOKLYN COLLEGE, Brooklyn, NY
B.A. in English Literature, 1982

SPECIAL SKILLS

Type 75 WPM, dictation, bookkeeping, word processing.

REFERENCES

Available on request

MILTON CARL CHAPMAN

64464 Collins Ave. #4B
Miami, FL 30392
305/555-7757

OBJECTIVE

Production assistant for a film company.

WORK EXPERIENCE

NEW ORDER PRODUCTIONS, Miami, FL
Production Assistant, 1989 - present
Assisted television producer and production coordinator.
Organized transportation for cast and crew members. Copied and
distributed scripts. Assisted location manager.

TERT FILM PRODUCTIONS, Chicago, IL
Production Coordinator, Summer 1988
Scouted locations; acquired film permits and props. Handled
airline reservations and accommodations for talent. Oversaw the
distribution of press releases. Photographed promotional stills.
Supervised crew and extras.

BALTIMORE FILM FESTIVAL, Baltimore, MD
Production Assistant, Summer 1987

Developed and coordinated special film series on forestry.
Assisted with the day-to-day operations of the film festival.
Contributed to promotional campaign.

KKSF RADIO, University of California, Berkeley, CA
Producer, 1987 - 1989

Served as an announcer on a weekly newscast. Edited copy for
newscast. Investigated and reported on student events.
Handled on-air coverage of local elections. Trained and
supervised new employees.

EDUCATION

UNIVERSITY OF CALIFORNIA, Berkeley, CA
B.A. in Film Production, 1989

REFERENCES PROVIDED UPON REQUEST

JOEL JAMES, III

1441 S. Goebert
Providence, RI   00231
401/555-1234
401/555-3782

Objective

President of a U.S. publishing corporation where I can apply my management, promotion and sales experience.

Employment History

JOHNSON PUBLISHING CORPORATION, Providence, RI
VICE PRESIDENT, 1980 - 1990

Promoted from Sales Manager to Vice President of Advertising after three years. Managed all phases of publishing properties including:

>   Furniture Magazine
>   Home Improvement Weekly
>   Scuba Digest
>   Travel Age Magazine
>   Pharmacy News

Established and developed the first newspaper advertising mat service in the furniture industry. Increased distributors and retailers using this service by 55% in three years. Improved the effectiveness and volume of all retail advertising.

REBUS PUBLISHING COMPANY, Boston, MA
ADVERTISING MANAGER, 1971 - 1979

Serviced and developed accounts throughout the eastern United States. Handled advertising for publications in the restaurant industry. Increased sales in my territories every year by at least 21%.

TIME MAGAZINE, New York, NY
ASSISTANT ADVERTISING PROMOTIONS MANAGER, 1967 - 1971

Spearheaded original promotion program that increased revenue 33% in two years. Developed new markets. Helped to improve company/customer relations.

ROYAL CROWN COLA CORPORATION, Chicago, IL
DIVISION SALES MANAGER, 1964 - 1967

Promoted from salesman to sales manager after one year. Organized sampling campaigns and in-store and restaurant displays. Directed bottlers' cooperative advertising and point-of-purchase displays.

JOEL JAMES, III - 2

Education

DRAKE UNIVERSITY, Des Moines, IA
B.A. in Economics, 1963
Graduated Phi Beta Kappa
Top 5% of class

Professional Affiliations

Rocking Chair, social and professional organization of the Furniture Industry
President, 1988 - 1990

Beverage Association of America
Board of Directors

Publishers Association
Advisory Committee

References

Available upon request

RITA WESTERBURG

3201 W. Oerono St.
Apartment 23
Pittsburgh, PA 28901
412/555-9302
412/555-4209

JOB SOUGHT: Public relations director for the marketing division of a major
candy manufacturer.

RELEVANT
EXPERIENCE: <u>Public Relations</u>

-Represented company to clients and retailers in order to present
new products.
-Organized and planned covention displays and strategy.
-Designed and executed direct mail campaign that identified
marketplace needs and new options for products.

<u>Management</u>

-Managed a sales/marketing staff which included account managers
and sales representatives.
-Monitored and studied the effectiveness of a national distribution
network.
-Oversaw all aspects of sales/marketing budget.

<u>Development</u>

-Conceived ads, posters and point-of-purchase materials for products.
-Initiated and published a monthly newsletter that was distributed
to current and potential customers.

EMPLOYMENT
HISTORY: <u>Redboy Peanut Crunch</u>, Pittsburgh, PA
National Sales Manager, 1987 - present
Account Manager, 1985 - 1987
Assistant Account Manager, 1984 - 1985
Personnel Assistant, 1982 - 1984
Receptionist, 1980 - 1982

EDUCATION: B.A. in English, 1979
University of Pennsylvania, Harrisburg, PA

SEMINARS: American Marketing Association Seminars, 1985 - 1990

SPECIAL
SKILLS: Computer literacy in BASIC and FORTRAN. Knowledge of WORD PERFECT 5
and DBASE-III.

REFERENCES: Available on request

GEORGE GHERING
329 Kedzie Ave.
Evanston, IL 60202
708/555-8487

OBJECTIVE: A position as an assistant advertising account executive.

SKILLS & ACHIEVEMENTS

* Coordinated media planning and buying
* Researched potential markets for ad campaigns
* Supervised artwork, layout and production
* Handled sales promotions
* Wrote original copy for ads
* Supervised trade shows and press shows
* Arranged and conducted sales meetings
* Designed marketing strategies
* Wrote and distributed press releases
* Acted as liaison to outside ad agencies

WORK EXPERIENCE

Advertising Coordinator, 1988 – present
Scandinavian Design, Evanston, IL

Assistant Coordinator of Advertising, 1982 – 1987
Marshall Fields, Evanston, IL

Assistant Sales Manager, 1980 – 1982
Rose Records, Skokie, IL

Salesperson, 1978 – 1980
Gemco, Inc., Chicago, IL

EDUCATION

B.A. in English, Northwestern University, 1978

SEMINARS

"Advertising in the 90's" – Northwestern University, 1989
"Account Management" – Loyola University, 1987

REFERENCES

Available on request

JEREMY CROMATINE, JR.

1700 N. FERN AVE.
APARTMENT 302
PITTSBURGH, PA   65420
412/555-3890   412/555-8902

CAREER GOAL

   Editor for a major publishing house

ACCOMPLISHMENTS

   *Researched and wrote book proposals.
   *Created and wrote advertising copy for book catalogs.
   *Developed two book ideas for book packaging company.
   *Wrote weekly local news column for local newspaper.
   *Edited manuscripts in preparation for publication.
   *Scripted five industrial films.
   *Handled paste-up and layout for ads.
   *Placed several articles in national magazines.
   *Edited five technical manuals for musical instruments.

EMPLOYMENT HISTORY

   RICHMOND PUBLISHING, Pittsburgh, PA
   Copywriter, 1985 - present

   SELF EMPLOYED, Madison, WI
   Freelance Writer, 1981 - 1985

HONORS

   Phi Beta Kappa, 1980
   Dean's List, 1979, 1980
   Donnelly Writing Contest, Honorable Mention, 1979
   Creative Writing Club, Founder, 1978 - 1980

REFERENCES

Available on request

CAROLINE NOE
5311 W. Cerritos Blvd.
Bloomington, IN 48331
417/555-9981

JOB OBJECTIVE

Public Relations Director

ACCOMPLISHMENTS

* Served local community and civic organizations as part-time public relations representative.

* Coordinated fund raising.

* Wrote successful grant proposals.

* Gathered and assembled information for news releases.

* Made appearances on local TV and radio programs.

* Wrote copy for promotional programs.

* Interacted successfully with public affairs representatives and the local media.

WORK HISTORY

Bloomington Press, Bloomington, IN
Advertising Assistant, 1988 - present

St. Andrews Children's Hospital, Bloomington, IN
Writer/Assistant Public Relations Director, 1988 - present

Indiana Auto Show, Indianapolis, IN
Public Relations Liaison, 1980 - 1987

McKinney For Congress, Indianapolis, IN
Assistant Fundraising Coordinator, 1984, 1986, 1988

EDUCATION

University of Mississippi, Jackson, MS
B.A. in English, 1972

REFERENCES

Provided upon request

CAROL BAKER
4420 Sunset Blvd.
Hollywood, CA 90027
213/555-9098

JOB SOUGHT: Promotion Director for a TV station.

SKILLS AND ACHEIVEMENTS

Promotion/Marketing

*Wrote and designed promotional pieces
*Evaluated content and direction of promotions
*Handled market research/demographic research
*Consulted clients on marketing plans

Video Production

*Handled shooting procedures, audio, lighting, casting and editing.
*Wrote and edited shooting scripts
*Determined production values for marketing accounts
*Oversaw postproduction and placement
*Coordinated presentations to clients

Media Planning

*Advised clients on media strategies
*Oversaw media budgets
*Determined and implemented marketing objectives
*Negotiated spot rates for clients

EMPLOYMENT HISTORY

Geary Advertising, Inc., Los Angeles, CA
Media Planner, 1984 - 1990

Goebert & Radner, Inc , Chicago, IL
Assistant Media Buyer, 1981 - 1984

Sears, Inc., Chicago, IL
Advertising Assistant, 1980 - 1981

EDUCATION

Drake University, Des Moines, IA
B.A. in Economics, 1980
Minor in Advertising
Phi Beta Kappa
Dean's List

References available on request

TALIA G. YOLIGA
15252 S. Vermont Ave. #231
San Diego, CA   91198

619/555-6000 (Day)   619/555-2496 (Evening)

CAREER OBJECTIVE:

Traffic Manager for an advertising agency.

SKILLS AND ACCOMPLISHMENTS:

*Oversaw all aspects of production and printing at a
national publication.
*Involved in heavy client and agency contact.
*Organized all art, mechanicals and final films with
stripping department.
*Handled in-depth media background contact with other media.
*Produced copy for ads.
*Conducted all in-store promotions and events.
*Place advertising and publicity in local publications.
*Consulted on grand-opening of Santa Monica store.
*Assisted customers frequently.

WORK EXPERIENCE:

ENTERTAINMENT WEEKLY MAGAZINE, Burbank, CA
Assistant Production Manager, 1986 - present

RADIO SHACK, INC, Hollywood, CA
Assistant to Promotion Director, 1982 - 1986

EDUCATION:

UNIVERSITY OF SOUTHERN CALIFORNIA, Los Angeles, CA
B.S. in Marketing, 1971

HONORS:

Cum Laude, 1971
Dean's List, 1970 - 1971
Goodman Sophomore Scholarship, 1969

References available upon request

CARRINE KANKA
9370 Torniquet Drive
Jackson, MS 73127

609/555-2909   609/555-3898

JOB OBJECTIVE

Science writer

SKILLS & ACCOMPLISHMENTS

--Edited <u>Save The Planet</u>, an environmental publication
directed at concerned citizens.

--Wrote articles for <u>Conservation</u> magazine.

--Contributed material to <u>Redbook</u> magazine.

--Wrote technical articles and instructional manuals on
software applications, office equipment and kitchen
appliances.

--Edited grant proposals for a local college.

EMPLOYMENT HISTORY

<u>Freelance Writer</u>, 1986 - present

EDUCATION

<u>Columbia University</u>, Columbia, SC
B.A. in Journalism, 1985
Minor in History

SPECIAL SKILLS

Ability to use a variety of computer hardware and software.
Working knowledge of French and German.

REFERENCES AND WRITING SAMPLES AVAILABLE

BEVERLY IOVINE
1723 LINCOLN PARK WEST
APARTMENT 3B
CHICAGO, IL 60613
312/555-2332

CAREER OBJECTIVE

Arts writer/reporter for a newspaper.

EXPERIENCE

*Wrote seven articles for series "Chicago Lithographers" for Chicago Artist magazine.

*Wrote four in-depth feature articles for Art Monthly.

*Wrote and illustrated a children's series for Youth Press. Subjects included: painting, music, film and poetry.

*Reviewed books and films for Lincoln Park Observer.

EMPLOYMENT HISTORY:

Freelance Writer, 1985 - present

Youth Press, Wilmette, IL
Writer/Illustrator, 1981 - 1984

Art Monthly, San Francisco, CA
Staff Writer, 1978 - 1981

EDUCATION:

Mills College, Oakland, CA
B.A. in English, 1970

HONORS:

Summa Cum Laude, 1970
Sandra Sanderson Writing Award, 1969

References and writing samples provided upon request

```
FRANK CARLSON
1400 3RD ST.  #189
NEW YORK, NY  10019
212/555-3494
```

JOB OBJECTIVE: Advertising agency art director.

SKILLS AND ACCOMPLISHMENTS:

--Oversaw all artwork at advertising agency.
--Held responsibility for hiring artists, researchers,
  copywriters and creative assistants.
--Conferred with clients regarding advertising strategy.
--Formulated design concepts.
--Assigned work to artists, photographers and writers.
--Produced general boardwork, illustrations, layouts, mechanicals
  for a department store chain and several ad agencies.
--Researched market for products.
--Conducted comparison studies with other products.
--Devised concepts for ads.
--Wrote copy for ads, flyers and inserts.
--Made sales presentations.

WORK
EXPERIENCE:

Terrence Harris Agency, New York, NY
Senior Art Director, 1982 - present
Staff Artist, 1980 - 1982

Carlson, Inc., San Francisco, CA
Freelance Commercial Artist, 1974 - 1980

Dandlor Corporation, Chicago, IL
Researcher/Copywriter, 1970 - 1974

EDUCATION:

Boston University, Boston, MA
B.A. in Advertising, 1973

Art Institute of Chicago, Chicago, IL
Summer 1972

REFERENCES:

Available upon request

JACK BISHOP

444 E. 17th St.   513/555-2909
Cincinnati, OH   58278   513/555-2999

OBJECTIVE

A career in television production.

ACCOMPLISHMENTS

TELEVISION PRODUCTION

*Served as assistant producer for local daily news magazine.
*Conducted interviews for stories.
*Scouted locations for filming.
*Oversaw crew on location.
*Supervised editing.
*Researched and developed story ideas.

REPORTING

*Cultivated contacts.
*Wrote stories about the local community.
*Researched and produced features on local politics.
*Conducted interviews.

FILM

*Edited videotape for local news magazine.
*Edited videotape for promotional programs.
*Filmed pieces for news show.

EMPLOYMENT HISTORY

Gruber Productions, Cincinnati, OH
Creative Director, 1988 - present

WCIN-TV, Cincinnati, OH
Producer, 1984 - 1988

KBLX Radio, San Francisco, CA
News Director, 1980 - 1984

Albuquerque News, Albuquerque, NM
Reporter, 1977 -1980

EDUCATION

Duke University, Chapel Hill, NC
B.S. in Journalism, 1977

References available on request

Sandra Fargo

589 Third Street
Bowling Green, KY 64490
502/555-4900 (Work)
502/555-3901 (Home)

JOB SOUGHT: Graphic Designer.

EDUCATION: <u>Colorado State University</u>, Denver, CO
                <u>Bachelor of Arts</u>, 1990
                Major: Visual Communications
                Minor: Graphic Arts
                Emphasis in visual communications concepts,
                corporate identity, environmental design,
                calligraphy, advertising, copywriting, offset
                lithography, compugraphics and silkscreening.

WORK
EXPERIENCE: <u>Colorado State University</u>, Denver, CO
                <u>Graphic Designer, Photography Studio</u>, 1989-1990
                Consulted with clients. Developed design
                concepts. Used compugraphic headliner and stat
                camera.

                <u>Rose and Co. Printers</u>, Denver, CO
                <u>Intern</u>, Summer 1989
                Gained experience in stripping, platemaking,
                pasting, halftone screening and use of stat
                camera.

                <u>Colorado State University</u>, Denver, CO
                <u>Media Center Intern</u>, 1989
                Assisted students and faculty in using various
                instructional media facilities.

                <u>Red Onion</u>, Sleepy Rock, CO
                <u>Waitress</u>, 1988-1990

MEMBERSHIPS: Art Directors of Denver
                Denver Women in Advertising
                American Design Council
                Delta Gamma Sorority

REFERENCES: Provided upon request

MARILYN CICCONE

1 S. Earl Road
Detroit, MI 33290
313/555-3434

OBJECTIVE

A management position in marketing/public relations.

WORK EXPERIENCE

BUBBA BURGER INC., Detroit, MI
Marketing/Public Relations Director, 1986 - present
Developed a successful marketing campaign for a fast food
restaurant chain. Initiated and maintained a positive working
relationship with radio and print media. Implemented marketing
strategies to increase sales at less profitable outlets.
Designed a training program for store managers and staff.

CHE COSMETICS CO., Harrisburg, MI
Marketing Representative, 1982 -1986
Demonstrated perfume products in specialty and department stores.
Reported customer reactions to manufacturers. Designed fliers
and advertising to promote products. Made frequent calls to
retail outlets.

CHEWY GUM, INC., Chicago, IL
Assistant to Sales Manager, 1977 - 1982
Handled both internal and external areas of sales and marketing,
including samples, advertising and pricing. Served as company
sales representative and sold gum to retail outlets.

EDUCATION

UCLA, Los Angeles, CA
B.A. Marketing, 1976

SEMINARS

Michigan Marketing Workshop, 1988, 1989
P.R. Association Seminars, 1984

References available on request.

JEFFREY SCOTT ROHN

9229 E. Adler Drive
Wheaton, IL 60089
708/555-4390 (Home)
708/555-2621 (Office)

OBJECTIVE: Editorial Assistant for Allstate Corporate
                Publications.

ACCOMPLISHMENTS:

Editing

--Redesigned <u>Discoveries</u>, a company publication, and turned
it into a visually and literarily stimulating magazine.

--Devised a system to maintain accurate mailing list.

--Oversaw layout and design of publication.

--Improved quality of paper and photography.

--Reduced costs while increasing readership.

--Persuaded employees to contribute articles for
publications.

Writing

--Edited and wrote articles for company publications.

--Wrote budget reports and grant proposals.

--Researched and wrote a report on software applications.

--Wrote a technical report on the feasibility of office
copying systems.

EMPLOYMENT HISTORY:

<u>Allstate Insurance Co.</u>, Northbrook, IL

Graphic Designer, 1985 - present
Editor, <u>Discoveries</u>, 1988 - present
Staff Artist, 1980 - 1985
Administrative Assistant, 1979 - 1980

JEFFREY SCOTT ROHN - 2

EDUCATION:

> <u>University of Wisconsin</u>, Madison, WI
> B.A. in Art, 1978
> Minor in English

SPECIAL SKILLS:

> Word processing, computer graphics, computer programming,
> working knowledge of Spanish.

REFERENCES:

> Available on request

JUAN C. GARCIA
2103 AFTON STREET
TEMPLE HILL, MARYLAND 20748
HOME (301) 555-2419

EDUCATION:

Columbia University, New York, NY
Majors: Communications, Business
Degree expected: Bachelor of Science, 1990
Grade point average: 3.0
Regents Scholarship recipient
Columbia University Scholarship recipient

EXPERIENCE:

7/89-9/89

Graduate Business Library, Columbia University, NY
General library duties. Entered new students and
books onto computer files. Gave out microfiche.
Reserved and distributed materials.

9/88-5/89

German Department, Columbia Univeristy, NY
Performed general office duties. Offered extensive
information assistance by phone and in person.
Collated and proofread class materials. Assisted
professors in the gathering of class materials.

6/88-9/88

Loan Collections Department, Columbia University, NY
Initiated new filing system for the office. Checked
arrears in Bursar's Office during registration period.

9/87-5/88

School of Continuing Education, Columbia University, NY
Involved in heavy public contact as well as general
clerical duties.

SPECIAL ABILITIES:

Total fluency in Spanish. Currently studying German.
Can program in BASIC. Excellent research skills.

REFERENCES:

Available on request

LUIS SANCHEZ

4742 N. Lawndale
Chicago, IL 60625
312/555-2574

OBJECTIVE: Video Production Assistant.

**WORK
EXPERIENCE:**   <u>Good's Video</u>, Chicago, IL
Assistant Manager, 1987 - present
Served as assistant manager of a full-service
video store with partial supervision of seven
salespeople. Researched customer's buying habits
and preferences. Handled promotion and mailings
for special sales and in-store events. Helped to
increase sales through personal attention to
customer needs.

<u>Johnson Florists</u>, Chicago, IL
Salesperson, 1980 - 1987
Sold flowers. Greeted customers and advised them
on their needs. Generated repeat business by
encouraging customers to return. Entered data on
computer to keep track of inventory. Handled
returns and orders from distributor. Designed
displays for store.

<u>Mita Co.</u>, Chicago, IL
Sales representative, 1975 -1980
Sold and serviced office copiers to businesses and
schools in the greater Chicago area. Maintained
good customer relations through frequent calls and
visits. Identified potential customers.

EDUCATION: <u>Northeastern Illinois University</u>, Chicago, IL
Attended two years. Majored in Film.

<u>Central High School</u>, Chicago, IL
Graduated 1980. Won amateur film award.

REFERENCES: Available on request.

DAVID GOTTNER

35666 Hialeah Ave. #6
Hialeah, FL 33333
305/555-2319 (H)
305/555-4700 (W)

Job Objective: Commercial artist for a major newspaper with the
career goal of media management.

Skills:

*Illustration
*Layout
*Paste-up
*Copywriting
*Research
*Photography

Accomplishments:

*Served as artistic consultant for various university
departments.

*Taught classes in commercial art at the college level, including
Principles and Technique of Layout, Paste-up, Linedrawing,
Advertising, Photography and Copywriting.

*Acted as advisor for campus newspaper.

*Designed and illustrated a literary journal.

Employment History:

Dade Community College, Miami, FL
Assistant Professor, Art Department, 1977 - present

Education:

Northwestern University, Evanston, IL
M.A. in Fine Arts, 1976

Pinkens College, Fort Briggs, MO,
B.A. in Art, 1975

References available

SHIRLEY G. BOTERN

7 Pine Knoll
Baltimore, MD   02293
301/555-5665

CAREER GOAL: A career in the production side of the film industry.

RELATED ACCOMPLISHMENTS

Film & Television

*Assisted television producer and production coordinator.
*Organized transportation for cast and crew members.
*Copied and distributed scripts.
*Assisted location manager.
*Scouted locations; acquired film permits and props.
*Handled airline reservations and accommodations for talent.
*Oversaw the distribution of press releases.
*Photographed promotional stills.
*Supervised crew and extras.

Radio

*Served as an announcer on a weekly newscast.
*Edited copy for newscast.
*Investigated and reported on student events.
*Handled on-air coverage of local elections.
*Trained and supervised new employees.

EMPLOYMENT HISTORY

SUNSHINE PRODUCTIONS, Baltimore, MD
Production Assistant, 1989 - present

CERES FILM PRODUCTIONS, Chicago, IL
Production Coordinator, Summer 1988

MIAMI FILM FESTIVAL, Miami, FL
Production Assistant, Summer 1987

WESM RADIO, University of Miami, Miami, FL
Producer, 1987 - 1989

EDUCATION

UNIVERSITY OF MIAMI, Miami, FL
B.A. in Film Production, 1989

REFERENCES PROVIDED UPON REQUEST

CHRISTOPHER T. SCHMIDTT
65 Drake Drive
St. Louis, MO 53190
314/555-2222

JOB SOUGHT: Account executive for a public relations firm.

SKILLS AND ACCOMPLISHMENTS:

   * Handled public relations activities for seven clients.

   * Developed product and service publicity.

   * Wrote and edited press releases.

   * Bought advertising space.

   * Scheduled news conferences.

   * Supervised a staff of three writers.

   * Oversaw budgets.

   * Organized company meetings.

   * Designed graphics.

EMPLOYMENT HISTORY:

1980 to present   Henry Stone Public Relations, St. Louis, MO
                      Public Relations Manager

1976 - 1980   Avenue Graphics, Chicago, IL
                      Graphic Artist

1969 - 1975   Mark Shale, Skokie, IL
                      Salesperson

EDUCATION:

1969   Northeastern University, Chicago, IL
                      B.A. in Biology

1974 - 1977   Art Institute of Chicago, Chicago, IL
                      Took evening courses in graphic arts

REFERENCES AVAILABLE

EUGENE T. SHOW

432 Sentinel Ave.
Kansas City, MO 74309
816/555-3903

OBJECTIVE: A career in advertising media services.

EDUCATION: STEVENS COLLEGE, Kansas City, MO

               B.A. in Advertising, June 1990
               Honor Society
               3.66 GPA in major field
               3.44 GPA overall
               Student Government Secretary
               Homecoming Committee

               Plan to pursue a Master's degree at a future date.

               EASTERN CITY HIGH SCHOOL, Portland, OR

               Graduated 1986
               Salutatorian
               President of Senior Class
               Drama Club
               Soccer Team

WORK
EXPERIENCE: ANDERS ADVERTISING, INC., Kansas City, MO
               Marketing Intern, Summer 1989
               Assisted Marketing Manager in areas of promotion, product
               development and demographic analysis.

               SURVEY SERVICE, INC., Kansas City, MO
               Telephone Surveyor, Summer 1987 & 1988

               RADICAL RECORDS, East Lydon, MO
               Salesperson, Summer 1986

SPECIAL
SKILLS: Working knowledge of German, French and Spanish. Familiarity
               with several computer software programs.

               References available

MARIO ROBERTO COLON
343 S. Evansville Ave.
Albany, NY 12908
518/555-2902

OBJECTIVE: A career in the communications industry, preferably
in public relations.

WORK EXPERIENCE:

Pollon Public Relations, Albany, NY
Public Relations Manager, 1980 - 1990

Handled public relations activities for seven clients. Developed
product and service publicity. Wrote and edited press releases.
Bought advertising space. Scheduled news conferences.
Supervised a staff of three writers. Oversaw budgets.

Michigan Graphics, Chicago, IL
Graphic Artist, 1975 - 1980

Oversaw accounts from concept through production. Logged
expenses. Approved layout. Contracted freelance artists.
Operated computerized typesetting equipment.

Shae Carpets, Pittsburgh, PA
Salesperson, 1969 - 1975

Handled both internal and external areas of sales and marketing,
including samples, advertising and pricing. Served as company
sales representative and sold carpeting to retail outlets.

EDUCATION:

Northeastern University, Chicago, IL
B.A. in Biology, 1969

Art Institute of Chicago, Chicago, IL
Took evening courses in graphic arts, 1974 -1977

REFERENCES AVAILABLE UPON REQUEST

MICHELLE CRUMLEY
2316 SHERMAN AVE. #3B
EVANSTON, IL 60201
708/555-4727

EDUCATION: Northwestern University, Evanston, IL
                      B.S. in Journalism
                      Expected June 1991
                      GPA: 3.45

HONORS: Phi Beta Kappa
                      Dean's List Seven Quarters
                      Owen L. Coon Award, Honorable Mention

ACTIVITIES: President, Activities & Organizations Board
                      Wa-Mu Show
                      Captain, Soccer Team
                      Freshman Advisor

WORK
EXPERIENCE: Evanston Review, Evanston, IL
                      Intern, Summer 1990
                      Assisted in layout, editing and reporting for local
                      newspaper. Wrote and edited articles. Handled preparatory
                      research for local election coverage.

                      Northwestern University, Evanston, IL
                      General Office, Registrar, 1988 - 1990
                      Processed transcript requests. Entered registrations
                      on the computer. Provided informational assistance to
                      students.

SPECIAL SKILLS: Knowledge of French & Russian. Experience using
                      WORDSTAR software.

REFERENCES: Available on request

PENELOPE PARSONS

140 E. 2nd Ave.
Apartment 3
Muncie, IN 66449
317/555-1188

JOB OBJECTIVE: A position as an editorial assistant for a
publishing company.

ACCOMPLISHMENTS:

Writing/Editing

*Wrote and edited manuals for signal processors and keyboards.
*Served as co-author for the book Gardening in the 80's.
*Edited funding proposals for local arts organization.
*Wrote an office procedures manual.
*Contributed articles to various magazine, newspapers and
periodicals.

Research

*Conducted political research for local political campaign.
*Handled background research for a book series.
*Collected data on office procedures for production of manual.
*Researched topics for magazine articles.

EMPLOYMENT HISTORY:

Freelance Writer, 1982 - present

BANK OF AMERICA, Muncie, IN
Staffing Director, 1987 - 1990

TORBERT'S FINE CLOTHING, Knoxville, KY
Sales Associate, 1982 - 1987

EDUCATION

SAN FRANCISCO STATE UNIVERSITY, San Francisco, CA
B.A. in Linguistics with a minor in English, 1981

REFERENCES

Available on request

CARLOS VEGA
548 W. Hollywood Way
Burbank, CA   91505
818/555-9090

PROFESSIONAL OBJECTIVE:

   An upper-level management position in the record industry where I can
   employ my promotion and marketing experience.

PROFESSIONAL BACKGROUND:

   Warner Bros. Records, Burbank, CA
   Director of Marketing/Jazz Department, 1988 - present
   Developed and implemented strategic marketing plans for new releases and
   catalog. Produced reissue packages and samplers, both retail and
   promotional. Created ad copy. Interfaced with creative services and
   national/local print & radio. Oversaw all aspects of sales. Coordinated
   promotional activities and chart reports.

   I.R.S. Records, Los Angeles, CA
   National Sales Manager, 1984 - 1988
   West Coast Sales Manager, 1981 - 1984
   Increased sales profile specifically west coast retailers, one-stops and
   racks. Promoted to National Sales Manager where I established sales
   and promotion programs for the company. Coordinated radio/chart reports.

   Specialty Records, Scranton, PA
   Sales Representative, 1980
   Handled sales, merchandising and account servicing for LPs and cassettes.
   Called on major chains and small independent retailers. Promoted new
   releases and maintained account inventory.

   Tower Records, Los Angeles, CA
   Manager, 1979 - 1980
   Handled sales, merchandising, customer service, product selection and ordering,
   personnel management and supervision for a full line retail outlet.

   MCA Records Distribution, Universal City, CA
   Sales Representative, 1973 - 1979
   Promoted and sold MCA product to Los Angeles and surrounding counties.
   Designed in-store and window displays. Coordinated media advertising
   support programs.

EDUCATION:

   Berkeley University, Berkeley, CA
   B.A., Liberal Arts, 1971

   References provided on request

RONETTE TAWANA JOHNSON

1750 N. Normandie Ave. #201
Miami, FL 33505
305/555-2922 (Home)
305/555-4000 (Office)

OBJECTIVE: A position at a commercial radio station.

SKILLS AND ACCOMPLISHMENTS:

   *Assisted in the management of a college radio station.

   *Helped to direct and supervise staff.

   *Established music format guidelines.

   *Wrote and edited budget proposals.

   *Assisted in financial matters.

   *Created and implemented new music format.

   *Planned and organized performances by artists at local
   venues in conjunction with the station.

   *Served as on-air personality.

   *Trained a staff of disc jockeys.

EMPLOYMENT HISTORY:

   WLVE-RADIO, Ft. Lauderdale, FL
   Assistant General Manager, 1989 - 1990

   WRDO-RADIO, Ft. Myers, FL
   Music Director, 1987 - 1988

   WWOP-TV, New York, NY
   Intern, 1989

EDUCATION:

   UNIVERSITY OF SOUTH FLORIDA, Ft. Lauderdale, FL
   B.A. in Broadcasting, 1990

   FT. MYERS COLLEGE, Ft. Myers, FL
   1986 - 1988

References provided on request

PAMELA SUE HUSPERS

Permanent Address: Temporary Address:
South East Hollow Road   150 Fort Washington Ave.
Berlin, NY 10951   New York, NY 10032
(518) 555-6057   (212) 738-2498

OBJECTIVE: A management trainee position in the telecommunications
                  industry.

EDUCATION: Bachelor of Science, Communications
                  New York University, New York, NY
                  Date of Graduation, May 1990
                  Communications G.P.A. 3.45
                  Academic G.P.A. 3.07

PROFESSIONAL
EXPERIENCE: V.I.T.A. (Volunteer Income Tax Assistance), Spring 1990
                  Provided income tax assistance to lower income and
                  elderly taxpayers who were unable to prepare returns or
                  pay for professional assistance.

                  Tutor, Self-employed, September 1988 - present
                  Helped students to better understand the basic concepts
                  and ideas of mathematics.

                  Randy's Seafood, New York, NY
                  Cook, Summer 1988
                  Prepared and cooked assorted seafood dishes. Accounted
                  for deliveries and receiving.

                  Jones Construction, Brooklyn, NY
                  General Laborer and Driver, Summer 1986-87
                  Operated heavy machinery and handled other aspects
                  of my job including delivering materials to and from
                  various job sites.

ACTIVITIES AND
HONORS: Beta Alpha Psi (Communications Honor Society), 1990
                  Dean's List, Fall 1988 & Spring 1990
                  A.I.S.E.C. - Association for International Business
                  Played on racquetball and tennis teams

REFERENCES: Available upon request

Christopher Knight
1700 W. Armadillo
San Diego, CA 90087
619/555-9000
619/555-2839

OBJECTIVE: To obtain a position as Vice President of Public Relations with an
           aeronautical corporation.

AREAS OF EXPERIENCE:

Marketing Development

        *Initiated and supervised sales programs for aircraft
         distributors selling aircraft to businesses throughout the
         western United States.

        *Managed accounts with a profit range of $100,000 to $1,000,000,
         including Dow Chemical, Landston Steel, Mercury Co., Berkeley
         Metallurgical & Ford Motor Co.

        *Demonstrated to customer companies how to use aircraft to
         coordinate and consolidate expanding facilities.

        *Introduced and expanded use of aircraft for musical tours.

Public Relations

        *Handled all levels of sales promotion, corporate public relations and
         training of industry on company use of aircraft.

        *Managed promotions including personal presentations, radio & TV
         broadcasts, news stories and magazine features.

Pilot Training

        *Taught primary, secondary and instrument flight in single and
         multi-engine aircraft.

Christopher Knight - 2

EMPLOYMENT HISTORY: <u>Hughes Aircraft, Inc.</u>, San Diego, CA
Sales Manager and Chief Pilot, 1981 - present

<u>Boeing Corporation</u>, Kansas City, MO
Assistant Manager of Promotion, 1972 - 1980

<u>American Airlines</u>, Dallas, TX
Pilot, 1965 - 1972

<u>United States Airforce</u>, Houston, TX
Flight Instructor, 1963 - 1965

PROFESSIONAL
LICENSE: Airline Transport Rating 14352-60
Single, Multi-Engine-Land
Flight Instructor - Instrument

EDUCATION: University of Texas, Houston, TX
B.A. in History, 1961

MILITARY
SERVICE: United States Air Force
1963 - 1965

REFERENCES: Available on request

SONDRA NIKE

1500 W. Redwood Drive #323
Salt Lake City, UT 83902
801/555-3921

OBJECTIVE

A career in the field of graphic design.

EDUCATION

Utah State College of Design, Salt Lake City, UT
Currently working towards a B.A. in Design; expected June 1991
Coursework includes: Advertising Design, Poster Design, Lettering,
Typography, Calligraphy, Printing & Photography.

Harper College, Palatine, IL
Attended two years, 1987 - 1988

EXPERIENCE

Utah State College of Design, Salt Lake City, UT
Designed Music Festival Poster (1990),program cover for Alumni
Association (1990), ads for the Design Club Convention (1989), poster
for Utah Singers appearance (1989).

Harris Drafting & Art Supplies, Arlington Heights, IL
Sold supplies to artists, architects and designers in the area.

AWARDS

Utah State College Design Show, Honorable Mention, 1990
Music Festival Poster Competition, First Place, 1990
Western Art Fair, Third Prize, Design Category, 1989
Dean's List, 1989. 1990

ACTIVITIES

Member of Utah Design Club
Member of Zeta Phi Sorority
Western Poster Design Workshop

REFERENCES

Available on request

MICHAEL E. MARLOW

4455 W. Gunderson
Berkeley, CA 91404
415/555-4909

JOB SOUGHT

A position in an advertising agency where I can use my graphic design skills.

EDUCATION

University of California at Berkeley, Berkeley, CA
B.A. in Visual Communications; degree expected, June 1991

Areas of concentration include: Graphic Design, Typography, Lettering, Package Design, Illustration, Photography, Calligraphy & Industrial Technology.

WORK EXPERIENCE

What's Hip Advertising, Inc., San Francisco, CA
Staff Artist, Summers 1989, 1990.

Handled concept development, design and layout, typesetting, and placement of ads for agency. Assisted in-house print facility with stripping, platemaking, binding and finishing.

Strange's Art Supplies, Berkeley, CA
Sales Assistant, Part-time, 1988 – present

Assisted students, artists and designer in the area with choosing art supplies. Handled cash deposits. Trained new employees.

HONORS

Earth Day Poster Competition, Honorable Mention, 1990
Berkeley Chamber of Commerce Design Show, Second Place, 1989
American Society of Magazine Designers Scholarship, 1988

ACTIVITIES

Berkeley Design Club, Secretary, 1989 – present
Designers in Progress, Member, 1988 – present
Gambo's Poster Design Workshop, Witchita, KS, 1989

REFERENCES

Provided on request

BELINDA CARLISLE

333 E. 20th St. #3   212/555-2902
New York, NY 10019   212/555-5200

OBJECTIVE: A management position in a publishing house.

**WORK
EXPERIENCE:**

COAST MAGAZINE, New York, NY
Regional Manager, 1985 - present
Oversaw administration, negotiation and
maintenance of exchange agreements and sales
promotion. Tracked market changes, with
responsibility for executing responses to
developments. Led magazine's Eastern edition
through a reorganization period. Planned and
implemented new editions in the South.

POPSON & CO., Jersey City, NJ
Sales Coordinator, 1982 - 1985
Managed ten field representatives. Handled
information dissemination and distribution. Co-
designed a full-color catalog. Placed advertising
in major trade publications. Promoted products at
trade shows. Maintained inventory status reports
and personnel records.

SPORT MAGAZINE, INC., San Francisco, CA
Distribution Assistant, 1980 - 1982
Developed new distribution outlets through cold-
calls and follow-up visits. Increased
distribution in my district by 45% over a three-
year period. Coordinated a direct mail program
that increased magazine subscriptions 120%.

MITA CO., Atlanta, GA
Sales representative, 1975 -1980
Sold and serviced office copiers to businesses and
schools in the greater Atlanta area. Maintained
good customer relations through frequent calls and
visits. Identified potential customers.

EDUCATION:

OHIO UNIVERSITY, Akron, OH
B.S. in Communications, 1974

BELINDA CARLILSE - Page 2

PROFESSIONAL
MEMBERSHIPS:

American Publishing Association
East Side Community Association
Jersey City Chamber of Commerce

SEMINARS:

"Publishing Strategies," Chicago, IL
"International Publishing," New York, NY

REFERENCES:

Available on request.

RUPERT FERN

2840 Forest Avenue #2
Rochester, NY 19229
716/555-9432

OBJECTIVE: A career in radio where I can utilize my previous
                experience, my communications skills and my
                interpersonal skills.

EXPERIENCE: **WEGR-RADIO**, Rochester, NY
                MUSIC DIRECTOR, 1984 - present
                Oversaw weekly selection of music. Served as
                liaison to record labels, music venues and
                artists. Supervised music assistants. Conducted
                music tests with the general public.

                WBGO-RADIO, Syracuse, NY
                ASSISTANT MUSIC DIRECTOR, 1980 - 1984
                Assisted program director with music selection and
                programming. Cultivated new record label and
                venue contacts.

                RATIO PRODUCTIONS, Chicago, IL
                PRODUCER, 1978 - 1980
                Produced various commercials for radio.
                Auditioned and selected actors, musicians and
                technicians.

                KUUT-RADIO, Seattle, WA
                PRODUCER/ANNOUNCER, 1970 - 1977
                Produced a Top 40 hit music show for radio.
                Served as announcer, as well as producer.
                Researched and selected music. Interviewed
                artists.

EDUCATION: **SYRACUSE UNIVERSITY**, Syracuse, NY
                M.A. in Broadcasting, 1968
                B.A. in Communications, 1966

REFERENCES: Available on request.

RENEE GYLKISON
8 E. Western Avenue
Houston, TX 75737
713/555-8098

JOB OBJECTIVE

A position as assistant manager of publishing company.

ACHIEVEMENTS

* Orchestrated market analyses and researched competition for reports to the district manager.
* Identified clients' needs and problems and assured them of personal attention.
* Prepared sales forecasts and sales goals reports.
* Resolved service and billing problems.
* Developed monthly sales plans which identified necessary account maintenance and specific problems that required attention.
* Delivered sales presentations to groups and individuals.
* Maintained daily sales logs and referral logs.
* Identified potential new clients and established new accounts.
* Increased client base by 50%.

EMPLOYMENT HISTORY

American National Books, Inc., Houston, TX
Assistant Manager, 1988 to present

Unico International, Dallas, TX
Sales Representative, 1985 - 1988

Red's Shoes, Omaha, NE
Salesperson, 1984 - 1985

Tex Mex Tacos, Austin, TX
Management Trainee, 1984

EDUCATION

Austin College, Austin, TX
B.A. in History, 1984

REFERENCES

Provided upon request

PETER GILBERT TOPSTER
5554 S. Cicero Ave.
Chicago, IL 60622
312/555-3399

OBJECTIVE: Freelance Writer.

ACCOMPLISHMENTS:

WRITING

   *Wrote the books <u>Rock in the 60's</u> and <u>Growing Up</u>.
   *Edited grant proposals.
   *Created a brochure on grants programs.
   *Published articles in various magazines.
   *Researched, edited and compiled study guides.
   *Served as editor for several book projects.
   *Published a company newsletter.

ADMINISTRATIVE

   *Drafted and edited correspondence.
   *Managed expense accounts.
   *Handled scheduling of appointments and preparation of
   course materials.
   *Maintained payroll and financial records.
   *Interviewed, selected and supervised work-study students.
   *Organized and monitored registration for Theater Center
   classes.

EMPLOYMENT HISTORY:

   USA Publishing Group, Chicago, IL
   Book Writer, 1988 - present

   American College, Evanston, IL
   Editor, Grants Department, 1988

   Seventeen Magazine, Omni Magazine, Rock Magazine
   Feature Writer, 1987 - present

   Royal George Theater, Chicago, IL
   Editor/Office Manager, 1985 - 1987

   Northwestern University, Evanston, IL
   Administrative Assistant, 1987 -1989

EDUCATION

   Northwestern University, Evanston, IL
   Bachelor of Arts with Honors in English, 1984
   Cumulative GPA: 3.76/4.00

References available on request

KEVIN WONG

5449 Magnolia Way #4B
North Hollywood, CA
818/555-7344

OBJECTIVE: Production assistant.

WORK EXPERIENCE

<u>SABER PRODUCTIONS</u>, Burbank, CA
<u>Production Assistant</u>, 1989 - present
Assisted television producer and production coordinator.
Organized transportation for cast and crew members. Copied and
distributed scripts. Assisted location manager.

<u>FEDER FILM PRODUCTIONS</u>, San Francisco, CA
<u>Production Coordinator</u>, Summer 1988
Scouted locations; acquired film permits and props. Handled
airline reservations and accommodations for talent. Oversaw the
distribution of press releases. Photographed promotional stills.
Supervised crew and extras.

<u>CHICAGO FILM FESTIVAL</u>, Chicago, IL
<u>Production Assistant</u>, Summer 1987

Developed and coordinated special film series on forestry.
Assisted with the day-to-day operations of the film festival.
Contributed to promotional campaign.

<u>KKBT RADIO</u>, University of Seattle, Seattle, WA
<u>Producer</u>, 1987 - 1989

Served as an announcer on a weekly newscast. Edited copy for
newscast. Investigated and reported on student events.
Handled on-air coverage of local elections. Trained and
supervised new employees.

EDUCATION

<u>UNIVERSITY OF SEATTLE</u>, Seattle, WA
B.A. in Film Production, 1989

REFERENCES PROVIDED UPON REQUEST

GEORGIA REBURN WEEKS

2213 Savannah Ave.
Apartment #2
Savannah, GA 30290   912/555-3930

OBJECTIVE: Program Director for a TV station.

WORK
EXPERIENCE:

    WGAR-TV, Savannah, GA
    ASSISTANT PROGRAM DIRECTOR, 1980 to present

    Oversaw daytime scheduling. Supervised a staff of fifteen. Coordinated
    all programs, commercials, public affairs announcements and news programs.
    Initiated programming changes that contributed to a significant rise in
    daytime ratings.

    WESM-TV, Harrisburg, PA
    PUBLIC AFFAIRS DIRECTOR, 1975 - 1980

    Created programs including a talk show and a news magazine. Served
    as host of a weekly public affairs program. Supervised a small staff.
    Oversaw various aspects of production.

    STAFF WRITER, 1970 - 1975

    Logged all promotional spots. Edited copy and tapes. Screened and
    processed trailers, slides and tapes.

EDUCATION:

    SAVANNAH UNIVERSITY, Savannah, GA
    M.S. in Communications, 1979

    DRAKE UNIVERSITY, Des Moines, IA
    B.A. in Broadcasting, 1968

MEMBERSHIPS:

    National Broadcasters Association
    Iowa Broadcasting Group

    References available

CLARENCE SCOTT TALLEY III
600 W. Porter St.
5
Las Vegas, NV 89890
702/555-3893

EDUCATION

<u>University of Nevada</u>, Las Vegas, NV
Bachelor of Arts in Communications
Expected June 1991

HONORS

Dean's List four semesters
Dornburn Scholarship
UNLV Communications Award

ACTIVITIES

President, Kappa Beta Fraternity
New Student Week Committee
Homecoming Planning Committee
Captain, Tennis Team

WORK EXPERIENCE

<u>Porter Rand & Associates</u>, Seattle, WA
Advertising Intern, 1990
Assisted sales staff in the areas of research,
demographics, sales forecasts, identifying new
customers and promotion.

<u>University of Nevada</u>, Las Vegas, NV
Research/Office Assistant, 1988-89
Researched and compiled materials for department
professors. Arranged filing system and supervisor's
library. Organized department inventory.

SPECIAL SKILLS

Experience using IBM and APPLE hardware and WORDSTAR
and dBASE III software programs.

References available

YOORI MATSUKA
Fulton Hall
2300 East Harrison
Room 306
Chicago, IL 60633
312/555-4849

OBJECTIVE:	A career in international communications.
EDUCATION:	University of Illinois at Chicago, Chicago, IL Bachelor of Arts in Communications. Expected June 1991
HONORS:	Phi Beta Kappa Dean's list five times Robeson Communications Scholarship, 1989
ACTIVITIES:	Vice President, Gamma Fraternity Freshman Advisor Homecoming Planning Committee Baseball Team Student Rights Group
WORK EXPERIENCE:	Westbrook Theater, Chicago, IL P.R. Intern, 1990 Composed press releases and public service announcements. Developed contacts with local columnists. Wrote ad copy for print and radio media. University of Illinois at Chicago Office Assistant, Journalism School, 1988-1990 Assisted with registrations, filing and typing. Arranged application materials. Assembled course packs. General Office, Registrar, 1988 Processed transcript requests. Entered registrations on the computer. Provided informational assistance to students.
SPECIAL SKILLS:	Hands-on computer experience using LOTUS 123 and dBASE III.
REFERENCES:	Available on request.

RUBIETTA WASHINGTON

453 Franklin Ave.
San Diego, CA 94890
619/555-3489

OBJECTIVE

A management position in public relations.

WORK EXPERIENCE

JUST PASTA INC., San Diego, CA
Marketing Director, 1986 - present
Developed a successful marketing campaign for a restaurant chain.
Initiated and maintained a positive working relationship with
radio and print media. Implemented marketing strategies to
increase sales at less profitable outlets. Designed a training
program for store managers and staff.

GREAT IDEAS CARPET CLEANING CO., Dallas, TX
Marketing Representative, 1982 -1986
Demonstrated carpet cleaners in specialty and department stores.
Reported customer reactions to manufacturers. Designed fliers
and advertising to promote products. Made frequent calls to
retail outlets.

REBO CHIPS, INC., Chicago, IL
Assistant to Sales Manager, 1977 - 1982
Handled both internal and external areas of sales and marketing,
including samples, advertising and pricing. Served as company
sales representative and sold potato chips to retail outlets.

EDUCATION

UNIVERSITY OF ILLINOIS AT CHICAGO, Chicago, IL
B.A. Marketing, 1976

SEMINARS

San Diego State Marketing Workshop, 1988, 1989
Sales and Marketing Association Seminars, 1984

References available on request.

RHONDA WARONKER

5320 Wilshire Blvd.
Los Angeles, CA 90069
213/555-9282

OBJECTIVE: Seeking a publicity/marketing position in the communications industry.

WORK
EXPERIENCE: WRT Records, Los Angeles, CA
Marketing Director, 9/88 - present
Handled distribution, retail marketing, advertising and mail order marketing. Wrote biographies and coordinated publicity. Obtained knowledge regarding domestic and overseas independent distribution, buyers for U.S. chain stores and Billboard reporters.

Hit Productions, Los Angeles, CA
Public Relations/Marketing Assistant, 5/87 - 9/88
Assisted PR Director with all duties, including radio promotion and retail marketing. Coordinated radio and print interviews for artists. Typing, filing and answering phones.

KTWV Radio, Los Angeles, CA
Music Director, 6/86 - 5/87
Selected appropriate music for a contemporary jazz format. Oversaw daily operations of music library and programming department. Supervised a staff of six.

EDUCATION: UCLA, Los Angeles, CA
B.A. in Arts Management, May 1985

ACTIVITIES: Phi Mu Alpha Music Fraternity, President
National Association of College Activities
Alpha Lambda Fraternity

SPECIAL
SKILLS: Working knowledge of Microsoft Word and Lotus 123.

References available on request.

SERITA TERESA WOODMAN
4553 N. Alamo Avenue
Dallas, TX 74667
216/555-8908

OBJECTIVE: Public relations representative for a company that
               markets vacation packages.

EXPERIENCE: <u>American Airlines, Inc.</u>, Dallas, TX
               Sales representative, 1988 - present
               Sold reservations for domestic flights, hotels and
               car rentals. Marketed travel packages through
               travel agencies. Negotiated airline and hotel
               discounts for customers. Devised itineraries and
               solved customers' travel related problems.

               <u>Salt Lake Travel</u>, Salt Lake City, UT
               Travel Agent, 1980 - 1988
               Handled customer reservations for airlines,
               hotels, and car rentals. Advised customers on
               competitive travel packages and prices.
               Interacted with all major airlines, hotel chains
               and car rental companies.

EDUCATION: <u>University of Illinois</u>, Urbana, IL
               B.A. in Anthropology, 1956

SPECIAL
SKILLS: Hands-on experience using most travel-related
               computer systems, including Apollo.

               Working knowledge of German, French and Polish.

REFERENCES: Available on request.

SAM SPRINGFIELD
666 Plymouth
Rd. #444
Bangor, ME
00099
207/555-4249

CAREER OBJECTIVE

A career in Graphic Design.

EMPLOYMENT HISTORY

Top Graphics, Bangor, ME
Graphic Designer, 1989 - present
Oversaw accounts from concept through production. Logged
expenses. Approved layout. Contracted freelance artists.
Operated computerized typesetting equipment.

Richmond Register, Richmond, VA
Production Manager, 1988 - 1989
Supervised staff of five designers. Coordinated typesetting
and camera schedules. Consistently met deadlines.
Coordinated advertising for daily and Sunday editions.
Maintained supply stock.

Staff Designer, 1987 - 1988
Designed and produced editorial and advertising layouts.
Developed and implemented ad strategies. Created
promotional materials.

Springfield Design, Bangor, ME
Freelance Designer, 1987- present
Produced posters, logos, brochures and ads for a variety of
companies and organizations.

EDUCATION

Bangor School of Design, Bangor, ME
Studied Advanced Compugraphics, Summer, 1990

University of Pittsburgh, Pittsburgh, PA
Bachelor of Arts in Design, 1986
Design Honor Award
Photography Honor Award

University of Hawaii, Honolulu, HI
Studied liberal arts, 1983 - 1984

References available upon request.

SANDRA L. PEARSON

12 E. Tenth St.
San Francisco, CA 94890
415/555-2343

JOB OBJECTIVE

A management position in cable television advertising sales.

RELEVANT EXPERIENCE

*Sold space in television for four major clients in the automotive industry.

*Served as a liaison between clients and television and radio station salespeople.

*Researched demographic and public buying habits for clients.

*Sold space for daytime programming on local T.V. station.

*Advised station on content and suitability of ads.

*Served as a liaison between station and those purchasing advertising space.

EMPLOYMENT HISTORY

Medialink Advertising Agency, San Francisco, CA
Television Space Sales, September 1985 - June 1990.

KTUT Television, Portland, OR
Television Space Sales, October 1983 - August 1985.

KFTF Radio, Berkeley, CA
Staff Sales Assistant, June 1981 - June 1983.

EDUCATION

B.A. in Communications, University of California at Berkeley, 1983.

HONORS

Seeger Award, Outstanding Communications Senior, 1983
Dean's List, five semesters
Salutatorian, Overland High School, Palo Alto, CA, 1979

REFERENCES PROVIDED ON REQUEST

QEERI TUJAMOTA
1290 W. Forest Ave. #4
Milwaukee, WI 55409   414/555-2029

OBJECTIVE: A position as a graphic designer.

EXPERIENCE

Regis Advertising, Milwaukee, WI
Graphic Designer, 1989-1990
Handled development of concepts. Consulted clients.
Prepared camera-ready art. Used stat camera.

University of Illinois, Chicago, IL
Graphic Designer, University Art Gallery, 1988-1989
Designed posters and brochures for art exhibitions.

University of Illinois, Chicago, IL
Art Director, University Publications, 1989
Compiled and edited visuals for publications.

University of Illinois, Chicago, IL
Graphic Designer, Media Center, 1987-1988
Oversaw concept development. Consulted clients on design
choices. Prepared camera-ready art. Used compugraphic
headliner and stat camera.

EDUCATION

University of Illinois, Chicago, IL
B.A. in Visual Communications, 1990
Course of study: publication design, corporate identity,
lettering, photography, kinegraphics, compugraphics and
packaging.

MEMBERSHIPS

ADAC, Milwaukee, WI
Midwest Design Coalition, Chicago, IL
Greenpeace, Milwaukee, WI

AWARDS

U. of I. Art Show, Best in Show, 1989

References available upon request

MARION ZARET
3333 W. 57th St.
Apartment 12E
Brooklyn, NY 12909
718/555-2323
718/555-4999

OBJECTIVE: Public relations director for Soft Drink Company.

WORK
EXPERIENCE: Coca Cola, Inc., New York, NY
                  National Sales Manager, 1987 - present
                  Account Manager, 1985 - 1987
                  Assistant Account Manager, 1984 - 1985
                  Personnel Assistant, 1982 - 1984
                  Receptionist, 1980 - 1982

                  Managed a sales/marketing staff which included account managers
                  and sales representatives. Monitored and studied the effectiveness
                  of a national distribution network. Represented company to
                  clients and retailers in order to present new products. Organized
                  and planned convention displays and strategy. Oversaw all aspects
                  of sales/marketing budget. Designed and executed direct mail
                  program that identified marketplace needs and new options for
                  products. Conceived ads, posters and point-of-purchase materials
                  for products. Initiated and published a monthly newsletter that
                  was distributed to current and potential customers.

EDUCATION: American University, White Plains, NY
                  B.A. in English, 1979

SEMINARS: American Marketing Association Seminars, 1985 - 1990
                  Coca Cola Internal Sales Workshops, 1986 - 1990
                  Soft Drink Industry Conventions

SPECIAL
SKILLS: Computer literate in FORTRAN and BASIC. Experience using
                  SOFTMATE and MULTIMATE software.

                  References available on request

RUPERT TERRANCE BARHAM, III

10089 SUNSET BLVD.
BRENTWOOD, CA   90078
213/555-8000
213/555-8383

EMPLOYMENT HISTORY

HOLLYWOOD MAGAZINE, Burbank, CA
Director of Operations, 1985 - present
Supervised 28 regional managers and offices with 454 employees.
Oversaw all local operations, including circulation, advertising
sales, promotion/marketing and $20 million salary and budget
administration. Increased ad sales by $8 million, a 20% increase
over three years.

Assistant to General Manager, 1978 - 1985
Coordinated all of magazine's configuration changes. Served as
operations liaison to Hollywood - The European Edition.
Initiated subscription sales programs and formulated marketing
strategies. Developed and implemented all edition modifications
in order to boost circulation and optimize advertising sales.

AMERICAN OUTDOORSMAN, Omaha, NE
Assistant Publisher, 1972 - 1978
Reduced magazine to standard size which resulted in a substantial
reduction in paper and production costs. Helped magazine to meet
the changing needs of readership and advertisers. Supervised an
office of eleven.

Advertising Manager, 1965 - 1972
Generated $250,000 in advertising revenues. Increased consumer
awareness of the magazine which led to increased sales -
circulation grew an average of 17% each year. Stabilized
downward trends in circulation.

WORLD MAGAZINE, Amherst, MA
Regional Manager, 1958 - 1965
Oversaw administration, negotiation and maintenance of exchange
agreements and sales promotion. Tracked market changes, with
responsibility for executing responses to developments. Led
magazine's Eastern edition through a reorganization period.
Planned and implemented new editions in the South.

RUPERT TERRANCE BARHAM, III - 2

EDUCATION

<u>COLUMBIA UNIVERSITY</u>, Columbia, SC
M.A. in Journalism, 1957

<u>TUSCON UNIVERSITY</u>, Tuscon, AZ
B.A. in History, 1956

PROFESSIONAL MEMBERSHIPS

West Coast Publishing Society
National Association of Magazine Publishers
Brentwood Chamber of Commerce

REFERENCES

Available on request

SAMUEL TRAVIS SHAVERS

15 E. Greenview St. #333
Richmond, VA 18978
804/555-3903

EDUCATION

University of Virginia, Richmond, VA
B.A. in Journalism, 1990

Hawkins Journalism Scholarship, 1987, 1988
Interned with WRCH-TV, Senior Year
Vice President, Senior Class

WRITING EXPERIENCE

* Served as Senior Editor of campus newspaper; selected articles; approved editorials; edited and wrote copy; supervised seven writers.

* Assisted in the editing of literary magazine Flight; proofread and edited copy.

* Researched stories for local television station.

* Wrote a weekly column for campus newspaper; actively pursued investigative reporting; handled events both on campus and in the local community.

* Created design and layout for 1989 Freshman Handbook; assisted with typesetting and offset printing of handbook.

WORK HISTORY

University of Virginia, Richmond, VA
Senior Editor, Campus Newspaper, 1989-1990
Editor, Flight, 1990
Designer, Freshman Handbook, 1989
Writer, Campus Newspaper, 1988-1989

WRCH-TV, Richmond, VA
Intern, 1990

MEMBERSHIPS

Association of College Journalists, 1989 - 1990
Virginia Literary Society, 1988

REFERENCES

Available upon request

WILARD PADDOCK
343 S. Pennsylvania Ave.
Washington, D.C.   02221
202/555-2347

JOB OBJECTIVE: Art Director.

WORK
EXPERIENCE:

Umbrella Advertising, Inc., Washington, DC
Senior Art Director, 1982 - present
Staff Artist, 1980 - 1982
Oversaw all artwork. Held responsibility for hiring artists,
researchers, copywriters and creative assistants. Conferred with
clients regarding advertising strategy. Formulated design
concepts. Assigned work to artists, photographers and writers.

Artworks, Inc., Scranton, PA
Freelance Commercial Artist, 1974 - 1980
Produced general boardwork, illustrations, layouts, mechanicals
for a department store chain and several ad agencies.

Parker & Parker, Inc., Chicago, IL
Researcher/Copywriter, 1970 - 1974
Researched market for products. Conducted comparison studies
with other products. Devised concepts for ads. Wrote copy for
ads, flyers and inserts. Made sales presentations.

EDUCATION:

Penn State University, Allentown, PA
B.A. in Advertising, 1973

Inglewood School of Design, Inglewood, CA
Summer 1973

Art Institute of San Francisco, San Francisco, CA
Summer 1972

REFERENCES:

Available upon request

EUNICE T. BODEANE
1221 E. Cambridge Ave.
Lynn, MA 02129
617/555-8800
617/555-9922

OBJECTIVE: A position as publicist with an arts organization.

WORK
EXPERIENCE: Boston Opera Co., Boston, MA
                  P.R. Assistant, 1986 - present
                  Composed press releases and public service announcements
                  which publicized Opera events. Developed contacts with
                  Boston entertainment columnists which resulted in extensive
                  coverage. Organized a calendar of advertising deadlines.
                  Wrote ad copy for print and radio media.

                  Sandra Watt Agency, Boston, MA
                  Editorial/P.R. Assistant, 1981 - 1986
                  Edited technical and literary manuscripts. Compiled a
                  directory of Boston editors and publishers for agency use.
                  Organized an educational workshop for local writers.

EDUCATION: Ithaca University, Ithaca, NY
                  B.S. in Advertising, 1980
                  Coursework included: Marketing Techniques, Advertising,
                  Corporate Public Relations, P.R. Techniques.

HONORS: Sigma Kappa Nu Honorary Society
                  Honors in Advertising
                  Dean's List
                  Myron T. Kapp Public Relations Award

ACTIVITIES: Student Government Representative
                  Homecoming Committee
                  Soccer Club

SPECIAL
SKILLS: Proficient on IBM hardware and Word Perfect 5 software.
                  Fluent in Italian.

                  REFERENCES PROVIDED IF NEEDED

SHARON KLEINBACH

9000 Inez Drive
Tacoma, WA 98899
206/555-2909

JOB OBJECTIVE

Assistant Director of Public Relations

SKILLS & ACCOMPLISHMENTS

Public Relations

*Prepared news releases.
*Maintained personal media contacts.
*Prepared and edited copy for brochures, ads and posters.
*Helped to develop advertising plans.
*Edited copy for newsletter.
*Prepared and distributed newsletter to patrons.
*Handled all booking for live entertainment.

Office Management

*Coordinated workshops and seminars on publicity.
*Handled group travel and hotel arrangements.
*Supervised an office staff of eight.
*Maintained business calendar.
*Organized staff meetings.
*Booked convention space.
*Prepared financial reports.

EMPLOYMENT HISTORY

PARK AMERICA, Tacoma, WA
Administrative Assistant to Director of Public Relations,
1986 - present

Office Manager, 1983 - 1986

EDUCATION

BROOKLYN COLLEGE, Brooklyn, NY
B.A. in English Literature, 1982

SPECIAL SKILLS

Type 75 WPM, dictation, bookkeeping, word processing.

REFERENCES

Available on request

REBECCA MORNEY
4440 E. 14th St.
Bronx, NY 10009
212/555-1298

OBJECTIVE: A career in advertising.

WORK
EXPERIENCE:

> BROADWAY MAGAZINE, New York, NY
> Assistant Production Manager, 1986 - present
>
> Oversaw all aspects of production and printing at a national
> publication. Involved in heavy client and agency contact.
> Organized all art, mechanicals and final films with
> stripping department. Handled in-depth media background
> contact with other media. Produced copy for ads.
>
> CRAZY AL'S, Brooklyn, NY
> Assistant to Promotion Director, 1982 - 1986
>
> Conducted all in-store promotions and events. Place
> advertising and publicity in local publications. Consulted
> on grand-opening of Santa Monica store. Assisted customers
> frequently.

EDUCATION:

> UNIVERSITY OF ILLINOIS, Champaign, IL
> B.S. in Marketing, 1971

HONORS:

> Cum Laude, 1971
> Dean's List, 1970 - 1971
> Dirk Toomey Scholarship, 1969

References available upon request

RUTH M. DAVID

572 FIRST STREET
BROOKLYN, NY 11215
(212) 555-4328

Education
Princeton University, Princeton, NJ
Degree expected: M.S. in Communications, June, 1990
Class Rank: Top Twenty-five Percent

Honors: Associate Editor, Communications Journal

University of Wisconsin, Madison, WI
B.A. in Political Science, May 1988

Honors: Dean's List
         Marching Band Drill Instructor, Section Leader
         Residence Hall Council President

Work
Experience
Boston Theatre Co., Boston, MA
P.R. Internship, 6/89-9/89
Composed press releases and public service announcements
which publicized theatre events. Developed contacts with
local entertainment columnists which resulted in extensive
coverage. Wrote ad copy for print and radio media.

Other Experience
Citizen Action Group, New York, NY
Field Manager, 6/88 - 9/88
Promoted citizen awareness of state legislative process
and issues of toxic waste, utility control and consumer
legislation. Demonstrated effective fund raising and
communication methods to the canvass employees. Developed
and sustained employee motivation and productivity.

University of Wisconsin, Madison, WI
Resident Assistant, Office of Residential Life, 8/86 - 5/88
Administered all aspects of student affairs in university
residence halls, including program planning, discipline
and individual group counseling. Directed achievement of
student goals through guidance of the residence hall
council. Developed and implemented university policies.

University of Wisconsin, Madison, WI
Staff Training Lecturer, 8/87 - 11/88
Conducted workshops for residence hall staff on counseling
and effective communication.

References
Available on request

DARRYL PANDY
3300 E. 17TH ST. #2
ST. LOUIS, MO 54098
314/555-8979

Job Objective

Seeking a career in copywriting for an advertising agency

Skills & Accomplishments

WRITING

* Wrote copy for specific demographics
* Designed ads for magazine, newspaper and display
* Assisted in the editing of copy for radio jingles
* Produced copy for newsletters and brochures

RESEARCH

* Advised on advertising strategies in light of competition
* Oversaw specific product research
* Made recommendation based on research which were accepted
* Created consumer profile studies

Employment Experience

PORTER & COOK, St. Louis, MO
Assistant Copywriter, 1986 - present

Education

WASHINGTON UNIVERSITY, St. Louis, MO
B.A. in Advertising, 1985

Honors

Dean's List, 1984, 1985
Cum Laude, 1985
Jerome T. Coppick Advertising Award, 1984

References

Available on request

DAVID THOMAS STIN
10001 W. Edina Ave.
Edina, MN 53989
612/555-5453

CAREER OBJECTIVE

    A challenging position as an artist for a small to mid-sized
    advertising agency.

EDUCATION:

    University of Minnesota, St. Paul, MN
    B.A. in Commercial Art, expected 1991

WORK EXPERIENCE

    Minneapolis Magazine, Minneapolis, MN
    Commercial Artist, Summers 1988 - present
    Produced line drawings for magazine ads, slides and
    promotional materials. Gained experience in watercolors and
    acrylics.

    University of Minnesota, St. Paul, MN
    Designer, University Publications, 1990
    Handled all aspects of production from layout to finished
    product. Designed boardwork, paste-ups and reproductions.

    University of Minnesota, St. Paul, MN
    Photographer, Daily Gopher, 1988 - 1990
    Took photos for university newspaper. Assisted in placement
    and layout.

WORKSHOPS:

    Illustration Workshop, Art Institute of Chicago, 1989
    Midwest Design Seminar, St. Paul, MN 1988

References available on request.

SANTI   4390 S. Finley   504/555-3903
NOLE   Baton Rouge, LA 20932   504/555-3892

CAREER OBJECTIVE

Graphic Design.

EDUCATION

University of Louisiana, Baton Rouge, LA
Bachelor of Arts, Graphic Design, June 1989
Emphasis: environmental graphics, corporate identity, packaging,
             publication design, television graphics, typography.

Indiana State University, Terre Haute, IN
1987 – 1988
Emphasis: illustration, screen printing, communication studies.

Terre Haute Junior College, Terre Haute, IN
1986

WORK EXPERIENCE

Baton Graphics, Baton Rouge, LA
Graphic Designer, 1989 – present

Baton Graphics, Baton Rouge, LA
Intern, Summer 1988

University of Louisiana, Baton Rouge, LA
Yearbook Art Director, 1988

Art Director, Emerge Magazine, 1988

Indiana State University, Terre Haute, IN
Graphic Artist, Student Publications, 1987

MEMBERSHIPS

Art Directors and Artists Club, 1989

AWARDS

Student Design Competition, First Place, University of Louisiana, 1989

REFERENCES

Available on request

SAM GARRISON

83 Main Place #3B
Portland, ME   04129
207/555-2321

OBJECTIVE: A position as an advertising assistant where I
can use my advertising, marketing and graphic
arts skills.

EDUCATION: University of Maine, New Brunswick ME
B.A. in Advertising, 1987
Major Fields: Advertising, Marketing, Graphic
Arts, Journalism, Business

HONORS: Summa Cum Laude, 1987
Dean's List

**WORK
EXPERIENCE:**   Lee J. Harris, Inc., Bangor, ME
Advertising Intern, Summer 1986
Handled four accounts for advertising agency.
Designed and laid out ads. Wrote copy. Assisted
with traffic control. Served as intermediary
between client and account executives.

Bangor Life Magazine, Bangor, ME
Advertising Assistant, Part-Time, 1985
Assisted in designing ads for magazine copy.
Computed ad sizes. Translated data from dummy to
production work-sheets and distributed for review.
Provided informational assistance to clients.

New Brunswick Daily, New Brunswick, ME
Free-lance writer, 1984 - 1986
Wrote feature articles on local community news,
including education, sports, politics and the
arts. Provided photos and illustrations in
support of various articles.

REFERENCES: Provided if requested.

ANN D. IMMEN

7009 Pinotta Drive South
Duluth, MN 61119
218/555-8393 (Day)
218/555-3839 (Evening)

OBJECTIVE: Copywriter for a full-service publishing company.

EMPLOYMENT
EXPERIENCE: Timber Publishing, Inc., Duluth, MN
                     Staff Copywriter, 1988 - present
                     Researched and wrote book proposals, including
                     sales letter, synopsis and sample chapters.
                     Created advertising copy for company's book
                     catalogs. Composed captions for illustrations and
                     side bars. Handled layout and paste-up. Edited
                     and rewrote manuscripts in preparation for
                     publication.

                     Ann D. Immen, Inc., Madison, WI
                     Free-lance Writer, 1984 - 1988
                     Edited five technical manuals on computer
                     software. Scripted four industrial films for
                     various food service companies. Developed two
                     book ideas and drafted sales proposals for a book-
                     packaging company. Wrote several articles that
                     were published in national magazines. Composed
                     copy for department store catalog.

EDUCATION: University of Wisconsin, Madison, WI
                     B.A. in English, 1984

HONORS: Phi Beta Kappa, 1984
                     Dean's List, 1983, 1984
                     Thomas Trumble Writing Competition,
                       Second Prize, 1983
                     Writing Club, Secretary, 1984

References available upon request

```
                        WINONA T. SIMPSON
                      420 W. Easterly Avenue
                      Indianapolis, IN  49091
                          317/555-1212
```

OBJECTIVE

A management position in marketing or public relations.

PROFESSIONAL ACHIEVEMENTS

Marketing/Public Relations

* Developed a successful marketing campaign for a video rental chain.
* Initiated and maintained a positive working relationship with radio
  and print media.
* Implemented marketing strategies to increase sales at less profitable
  stores.
* Designed a training program for store managers and staff.

Promotion

* Demonstrated electronic equipment in stereo and department stores.
* Reported customer reactions to manufacturers.
* Designed fliers and advertising to promote products.
* Made frequent calls to retail outlets.

EMPLOYMENT HISTORY

Blockbuster Video, Inc., Indianapolis, IN
P.R. Director, 1985 - present

Jeron Stereo, Bloomington, IN
Marketing Representative, 1982 - 1985

Kader Advertising, St. Louis, MO
P.R. Assistant, 1980 - 1982

EDUCATION

Washington University, St. Louis, MO
B.S. in Education, 1980

HONORS

Phi Beta Kappa, 1980
Top 5% of class
Dean's List

REFERENCES

Provided on request

Chapter Six

SAMPLE COVER
LETTERS

ROSEMARY DEBORAH PARKER
5509 E. George St. #442
Columbia, SC 29263
803/555-2893

November 19, 1990

Septimus J. Harper
Publisher
Time Magazine
1 Rockefeller Plaza
New York, NY 10019

Dear Mr. Harper:

Please consider me for the position of editor for your magazine.

I have spent the past seven years as assistant editor of Carolina Woman
where I have handled a variety of challenging tasks. During this time,
I evaluated manuscripts, handled copy editing and rewriting, worked with
artists and designers on layout aspects and supervised the publication of
a poetry anthology. Previous to my tenure at Carolina Woman, I served as
copy editor for the Raleigh Gazette.

I have a B.A. in Journalism from Columbia University where I graduated
Summa Cum Laude in 1981.

Time would be a wonderful opportunity for me. I believe that I would be
a great asset to your publication. Please contact me for an interview at
your convenience.

Sincerely,

Rosemary Deborah Parker

terri franks
15 nob hill
san francisco, ca   91405
415/555-4398

Gilbert Secor, President
Unicorn Design, Inc.
2442 Market St.
Suite 4C
San Francisco, CA   91407

Dear Mr. Secor:

I am interested in applying for the position of graphic designer which
recently opened up in your company. For this purpose, I am enclosing
my resume for your perusal.

I am a recent graduate of the Berkeley College of Design where I received
a B.A. in Graphic Design. My areas of concentration included photography,
publication design, copywriting, typography and packaging. I also earned
a B.A. in History from the University of Minnesota in 1979.

My design experience includes the designing of ads, brochures and posters,
coordinating of fashion shows and creating business systems. I have
worked as a graphic design intern at Berkeley and as a graphics assistant
at Fern Labs in Palo Alto.

After several years as a homemaker and mother, I decided to pursue this
field. Now that I have earned my degree and gained the needed experience,
I am ready for the challenge of a position at a company such as yours.

I would like to show you my portfolio. Please feel free to call me for an
interview at your convenience.

Sincerely,

terri franks

10/26/90

KKBT Radio
5600 Sunset Blvd.
Los Angeles, CA   90028
Attn: Liz Kiley, Operations Manager

Dear Ms. Kiley:

This letter is in response to your ad in Radio and Records for a program director. I've been paying close attention to your station's recent changes in programming and was excited to hear that you have gone urban.

I have had extensive experience in the world of radio over the past fifteen years. I have served in a variety of capacities, including program director/music director at WROB in Robinson, IL, producer/ announcer at WGAU in Augusta, GA and producer/announcer for WREE in East St. Louis, IL. I am a graduate of the Midwest School of Broadcasting. Though my background has been in smaller radio markets, I feel I am ready to break into a major market.

Enclosed is my resume. Please take a look at it and let me know if I can see you for an interview. I'll be contacting you shortly.

Thank you for your time and consideration.

Sincerely,

Michael Ervin McDonald
333 E. Rhett Drive
Augusta, GA   33209
404/555-2108

MARTHA WAYANS
4500 77th St.
New York, NY   10032
212/555-3839

August 28, 1990

George Jacobs
Human Resources
AT&T
1200 E. 5th Ave.
New York, NY   10019

Dear Mr. Jacobs:

Mitchell Sanderson, who works in the sales department at AT&T, suggested that I contact you regarding a possible opening in your public relations department. I am enclosing my resume for your consideration.

I will be graduating this month from New York University with a degree in Communications. My recent induction into the Communications Honor Society (Beta Alpha Psi) was a personal milestone. I am also a member of the Association of International Business (A.I.B.).

I am interested in working in the communications industry in the field of public relations and I feel that the best place for me to start would be at AT&T.

I will be calling you in about a week to follow up on this letter. Please feel free to call Mr. Sanderson for a reference.

Sincerely,

Martha Wayans

June 12, 1991

Thomas Hardy
Director of Grants
Fernwood College
555 Colfax Ave.
Evanston, IL 60201

Dear Mr. Hardy:

This letter is in response to your ad in the <u>Evanston Review</u> for an editor for your grants department. I am enclosing my resume and writing samples for your review.

I have been working as a freelance writer for the past several years and my credits include authoring two books, serving as an editor for an arts magazine, the publication of various magazine articles and compiling and editing study guides for a local theater.

I graduated from Northwestern University, Phi Beta Kappa with honors in English. While at Northwestern, I received the Mayo Writing Prize and served as editor of a creative writing journal published by the university.

I believe I am qualified for the editor's position and I hope you agree with me after reviewing my accomplishments. I look forward to hearing from you soon.

Sincerely,

Geoffrey Hodges
329 Kedzie Ave. #2
Evanston, IL 60202
708/555-4727

CLARENCE SCOTT TALLEY III
600 Porter St.
Las Vegas, NV 89890
702/555-3893

May 15, 1991

Tabu Rebu
Creative Director
Quest Advertising, Inc.
2330 W. Delaney Blvd.
Los Angeles, CA 90029

Dear Mr. Rebu:

This is a letter of inquiry. I am curious to know whether there are any openings in your agency at the present time?

I expect to graduate in June from the University of Nevada with a Bachelor of Arts in Communications and I am looking towards a career in the advertising industry. While at Nevada, I was awarded the Dornburn Scholarship, received the Communications Award and made the Dean's List four times.

Last summer, I served as an advertising intern for Porter Rand & Associates. There I assisted the sales staff in the areas of research, demographics, sales forecasts and promotion. The experience gained in this internship, along with my degree, will serve as the foundation for my career in advertising.

Please review my resume and contact me if you have any openings currently. Thank you.

Sincerely,

Clarence Scott Talley III

MARLENE DRAKE
3300 Bay Road
Green Bay, WI 55390
414/555-4930

October 28, 1990

Derek Nord
Manager, Wardrobe Dept.
NBC
3300 Alameda Drive
Burbank, CA 91505

Dear Mr. Nord:

I will be arriving in Los Angeles in late November to begin my search for a job in the field of wardrobe. I will be relocating to the area early next year.

As you can see from my enclosed resume, I have extensive wardrobe experience. I worked for WWGB-TV as a wardrobe mistress and have handled the wardrobe for several bands in the Green Bay area. I have also gained experience with wardrobe in film and video.

I would especially like to meet with you while I am in town to discuss any possible openings you may have in your wardrobe department.

If I don't hear from you before I arrive in Los Angeles, I will call you when I do arrive. I look forward to meeting with you soon.

                              Sincerely,

                              Marlene Drake

November 1, 1990

Peter Sauers
Managing Director
Sauers Productions, Inc.
550 Magnolia Way
Burbank, CA 91501

Dear Mr. Sauers:

This letter is to inquire into the possibility of an opening in
your production company for a production assistant.

I have spent the last year working in Miami for New Order
Productions as a production assistant. I have benefitted greatly
from this experience, but it has always been my dream to work in
the Hollywood film industry. Hence, this letter. Last summer,
I served as production coordinator for Tert Films in Chicago and
the summer before as production assistant for the Baltimore Film
Festival. I received a B.A. in Film Production from the
University of Florida in 1989.

It is my long-term goal to become a director of films and I feel
that a position with your company would be an excellent beginning
for me.

I will follow this letter with a phone call. I look forward to
meeting with you.

                              Sincerly,

                              Milton Carl Chapman
                              66446 Collins Ave. #4B
                              Miami, FL 30309
                              305/555-2930
                              305/555-2992

3338 W. Redbook Drive
Amarillo, TX 78088
806/555-1910

January 2, 1991

Miles Franks
Director of Human Resources
WWTD-TV
4440 Peach Tree Avenue
Dallas, TX 78229

Dear Mr. Franks:

A mutual friend, Terrence Weber, informed me that you are looking for a new Director of Traffic for your TV station. I am interested in applying for this job. Enclosed is my resume.

As Assistant Director of Traffic at WARM-TV in Amarillo, I have acted as contact between syndication companies and the station, created logs, established sales availabilities and screened and processed tapes and films. I have held this position since 1987. Previous to my tenure at WARM-TV, I held the same position at WPIX-TV in El Paso where I was promoted from Assistant to Head Programmer.

I believe that my seven years experience well qualifies me for the next logical step in my career - Director of Traffic.

I would be happy to meet with you at any time. Please contact me at your earliest convenience.

Sincerely,

Harrison Crumpet
3338 W. Redbook Drive
Amarillo, TX 78077
806/555-1910

April 23, 1991

Rupert Goebert
Director
Santa Barbara Art Fair
6660 Forest Green Ave.
Santa Barbara, CA   92299

Dear Mr. Goebert:

I am interested in applying for the position of photographer for the 1991 Santa Barbara Art Fair. I learned of the position from your posting at the civic center.

My photography experience includes a stint as official photographer for the Nevada State Fair last year where I headed a team of photographers. I have worked with 35mm and 2 1/4 x 2 1/4 inch cameras along with video equipment. I have photographed for products, promotions, press releases and publications. I believe that my background qualifies for this position.

I am a graduate of the University of Washington in Tacoma where I earned a degree in Graphic Arts with a minor in Photography. I also have experience as a graphic designer.

Enclosed is my resume and a few samples of my photography. I will be in touch with you next week regarding this letter.

Sincerely,

Peter Klept
554 Grambling Road
Santa Barbara, CA   97770
815/555-2332

January 30, 1990

Robert T. Beatty
Director of Personnel
Turner Broadcasting Co.
One Turner Plaza
Atlanta, GA 33203

Dear Mr. Beatty:

I am writing to you regarding the possibilty of obtaining a position
within your company in the area of advertising sales.

I have several years of sales experience behind me, including work for
Medialink Advertising Agency in San Francisco and KTUT-TV in Portland.
As you can see from my resume, I have sold space for major clients in
the automotive industry, advised on the content and suitability of ads,
and have done demographic research.

My desire at this time is to break into cable television because I believe
it has a bright future and I want to be a part of that future. Please
review my resume and advise as to the feasibility of an interview.

Sincerely,

Sandra T. Pearson
12 E. Tenth St.
San Francisco, CA 94890
415/555-2343

May 15, 1991

Deborah Klugh
Director of Human Resources
ABC
11 Rockefeller Plaza
New York, NY 10019

Dear Ms. Klugh:

This letter is in response to your ad in <u>The New York Times</u> for a P.R. assistant. Enclosed are my resume and salary requirements as requested in the ad.

Next month I will be graduating from Boston University with a degree in Communications and a concentration in Public Relations. I was inducted into Phi Beta Kappa this month and expect to graduate with honors in June.

I am interested in working in the television industry and would be most pleased to be a part of the ABC team. I possess strong written and verbal communications skills and feel certain that I would do an excellent job in meeting the demands of this position.

Please contact me if you are interested. I am willing to travel to New York for an interview if necessary. Thank you for your time and consideration.

Sincerely,

Barton T. Quigley
Boston University
Fenton Hall
199 W. Hampshire Way
Boston, MA 02201
617/555-3839

February 19, 1991

Q.T. Wollers
Tatum Advertising Agency
555 Paddington Avenue
Boston, MA 02214

Dear Ms. Wollers:

   I am writing to inquire as to whether there are any openings in your
agency for a graphic artist.

   Currently, I manage the advertising department of the New England News
where I conceive and design ads, oversee development, layout and typesetting
and maintain the financial records and accounts of the department. While
I find my current position quite challenging, my first love and long-term
goal is graphic design. This is the reason for my interest in Tatum.

   I have a solid educational background in the field of design, including
an M.A. in Graphic Design from the Cambridge School of Design and a B.A. in
Visual Communications from the University of Chicago.

   Please review the enclosed resume and let me know whether you are
hiring at the present time.

                    Sincerely,

                    Teresa Morbito
                    15 Fourth St. East
                    Boston, MA 02115
                    602/555-4009

January 14, 1991

Gekko Publishing, Inc.
1700 Avenue of Industry
Dallas, TX 78989
Attn: Ricardo Montoya,
       Director of Personnel

Dear Mr. Montoya:

This letter is a response to your advertisement in Houston Chronicle's
classified section. The position of assistant manager of operations for
a publisher of Gekko's stature is one that appeals to me greatly. I am
enclosing my resume for your consideration in light of this opening.

Currently, I am assistant manager for a small, but dynamic publisher
in Houston - American National Books, Inc. My experience at American
National includes orchestrating market analyses, identifying client's needs
and meeting them, account maintenance and the establishing of new accounts.
Previous to this position, I served as a sales representative for Unico
International in Dallas.

I am willing to come to Dallas for an interview at your convenience.
Coming back to work in Dallas is something I am looking foward to. It's
a wonderful city.

Please feel free to contact me at either phone number listed below. I
look forward to meeting you and discussing this opportunity.

Sincerely,

Renee Gylkison
8 E. Western Avenue
Houston, TX 75737
713/555-8098
713/555-6000

WINONA T. SIMPSON
420 W. Easterly Avenue
Indianapolis, IN 49091

September 2, 1990

Thomas E. Eagletender
Pizza Hut, Inc.
4200 Bolt Ave.
Indianapolis, IN 48902

Dear Mr. Eagletender:

David Porter of your marketing department informed me that you were looking for a new P.R. manager for your midwest office. Therefore, I am sending along my resume for your consideration in regards to this position.

Currently, I serve as P.R. Director for Blockbuster Video in Indianapolis where I have been since 1985. Before that I worked as marketing representative for Jeron Stereo and as P.R. assistant for Kader Advertising.

My accomplishments include developing a successful marketing campaign for Blockbuster, implementing marketing strategies to increase sales at less profitable outlets and designing a training program for store managers and staff.

I believe my resume speaks for itself. I would very much like to meet with you to discuss this position further. Please contact me at 317/555-1212 at your convenience.

Sincerely,

Winona T. Simpson

BELINDA CARLISLE
333 E. 20th St. #3
New York, NY 10019
212/555-2902

December 2, 1990

Corlis Fenett, Jr.
President
Venture Publishing Corp.
7 Rockefeller Plaza
New York, NY 10019

Dear Mr. Fenett:

As regional manager of Coast Magazine, I have faced many
challenges and have handled each of them thoroughly, responsibly
and efficiently. Coast has benefitted greatly through my efforts
during the past seven years. In this position, I oversee
administration, negotiation and maintenance of exchange
agreements and promotion. I have led the magazine's Eastern
edition through a difficult reorganization period and planned and
implemented new editions in the South.

I have enjoyed my tenure at Coast, but I feel it is time to move
on to a new challenge. This challenge I hope to be the position
of Director of Operations at Venture Publishing Corp. I learned
of this opening from a fellow colleague in publishing.

Enclosed is my resume. Please review it and contact me if you
are interested. I am confident that you will be.

                    Sincerely,

                    Belinda Carlisle

3300 E. 17th St. #2
St. Louis, MO 54098
314/555-8979

Richard T. Yori
Director of Personnel
Sandler & Grey
333 N. Michigan Ave.
Chicago, IL 60601

Dear Mr. Yori:

I am writing to inquire about possible openings in your agency for
a copywriter.

Currently, I work as an assistant copywriter for Porter & Cook in St.
Louis, but I am looking to move on to a position of copywriter. My
experience includes writing copy for specific demographics, editing copy
for radio jingles, producing copy for newsletter and brochures and
specific product research. I feel that the experience gained in the last
four years at Porter & Cook well qualify me for the position of copywriter.
I graduated from Washington University Cum Laude with a B.A. in
Advertising.

Enclosed is my resume. If you have no openings at the present time
please keep me in mind for the future. Thank you.

Sincerely,

Darryl Pandy

December 13, 1990

Hollywood Reporter
Box 1140-H
465 Hollywood Way
Burbank, CA 91505

To Whom It May Concern:

I am responding to your ad in The Hollywood Reporter that ran 12/8/90 for a public relations assistant at a major Hollywood production company. I am enclosing my resume and salary requirements as requested.

I am a recent graduate of California State University at Northridge where I received a B.A. in Communications. My work includes an internship at Warner Bros. Studios in Burbank in the public relations department. My goal is a career in public relations in the entertainment industry.

I am anxious to learn more about this position and look forward to hearing from you soon. Please feel free to call me at home or at work. Thank you for your time and consideration.

Sincerely,

Ken Phillips
4000 Sunset Blvd.
Los Angeles, CA 90028

213/555-7648 (Home)
213/555-2000 (Work)

October 17, 1990

David D. Geras
Director of Broadcast Operations
WGN-TV
700 W. Addison
Chicago, IL 60625

Dear Mr. Geras:

I enjoyed meeting and speaking with you at the Broadcast Careers seminar at Howard University last spring. I am writing to you now to express my interest in an opening at WGN for a News Assistant. I am enclosing my resume for your review.

Besides my recent B.A. degree in Journalism, I have gained experience over the last four summers in a variety of workplaces. Most recently, I completed an internship at WDC-TV in Washington, DC where I assisted in the production of a news show. Previous internships include <u>Capitol Magazine</u>, <u>Chattanooga News</u> and Park Advertising, Inc.

I would be glad to come to Chicago for an interview at your convenience. Thank you for your time and consideration.

Sincerely,

Terri Bakkemo
700 Thornborough Rd.
Chattanooga, TN 75221
615/555-2111

February 12, 1991

Wendell C. Wilkerson
Editor
Richmond Register
330 S. Potomac Drive
Richmond, VA 11980

Dear Mr. Wilkerson:

I am writing in response to your opening for a beat reporter which was posted at the career office at the University of Virginia. I am currently seeking a position in the field of journalism and wish to be considered for this opening.

I graduated last June with a B.A. in Journalism from the University of Virginia. My writing/reporting experience includes a stint as Senior Editor of the campus newspaper, editing of a literary magazine and a broadcast journalism internship with WRCH-TV all right here in Richmond.

My enclosed resume details my experience. I believe that I am ready for this challenge. I am available for an interview at your convenience.

Thank you for considering me.

Sincerely,

Samuel Travis Shavers
15 E. Greenview St. #333
Richmond, VA 18978
804/555-3903

VGM CAREER BOOKS

CAREER DIRECTORIES
Careers Encyclopedia
Dictionary of Occupational Titles
Occupational Outlook Handbook

CAREERS FOR
Animal Lovers
Bookworms
Computer Buffs
Crafty People
Culture Lovers
Environmental Types
Film Buffs
Foreign Language Aficionados
Good Samaritans
Gourmets
History Buffs
Kids at Heart
Nature Lovers
Number Crunchers
Sports Nuts
Travel Buffs

CAREERS IN
Accounting; Advertising; Business; Child
Care; Communications; Computers;
Education; Engineering; Finance;
Government; Health Care; High Tech;
Law; Marketing; Medicine; Science;
Social & Rehabilitation Services

CAREER PLANNING
Beginning Entrepreneur
Career Planning & Development for
    College Students & Recent Graduates
Careers Checklists
Cover Letters They Don't Forget
Executive Job Search Strategies
Guide to Basic Resume Writing
Joyce Lain Kennedy's Career Book
Slam Dunk Resumes
Successful Interviewing for College
    Seniors

HOW TO
Approach an Advertising Agency and
    Walk Away with the Job You Want
Bounce Back Quickly After
    Losing Your Job
Change Your Career
Choose the Right Career
Get & Keep Your First Job
Get into the Right Law School
Get People to Do Things
    Your Way
Have a Winning Job Interview
Jump Start a Stalled Career
Land a Better Job
Launch Your Career in TV News
Make the Right Career Moves
Market Your College Degree
Move from College into a
    Secure Job
Negotiate the Raise
    You Deserve
Prepare a *Curriculum Vitae*
Prepare for College
Run Your Own Home Business
Succeed in College
Succeed in High School
Write Successful Cover Letters
Write a Winning Resume
Write Your College
    Application Essay

OPPORTUNITIES IN
Accounting
Acting
Advertising

Aerospace
Agriculture
Airline
Animal & Pet Care
Architecture
Automotive Service
Banking
Beauty Culture
Biological Sciences
Biotechnology
Book Publishing
Broadcasting
Building Construction Trades
Business Communication
Business Management
Cable Television
CAD/CAM
Carpentry
Chemistry
Child Care
Chiropractic
Civil Engineering
Cleaning Service
Commercial Art & Graphic Design
Computer Maintenance
Computer Science
Counseling & Development
Crafts
Culinary
Customer Service
Data Processing
Dental Care
Desktop Publishing
Direct Marketing
Drafting
Electrical Trades
Electronic & Electrical Engineering
Electronics
Energy
Engineering
Engineering Technology
Environmental
Eye Care
Fashion
Fast Food
Federal Government
Film
Financial
Fire Protection Services
Fitness
Food Services
Foreign Language
Forestry
Government Service
Health & Medical
High Tech
Home Economics
Homecare Services
Hospital Administration
Hotel & Motel Management
Human Resource Management
Information Systems
Installation & Repair
Insurance
Interior Design
International Business
Journalism
Laser Technology
Law
Law Enforcement & Criminal
    Justice
Library & Information Science
Machine Trades
Magazine Publishing
Marine & Maritime
Masonry
Marketing
Materials Science
Mechanical Engineering
Medical Imaging
Medical Technology

Metalworking
Military
Modeling
Music
Newspaper Publishing
Nonprofit Organizations
Nursing
Nutrition
Occupational Therapy
Office Occupations
Packaging Science
Paralegal
Paramedical
Part-time & Summer Jobs
Performing Arts
Petroleum
Pharmacy
Photography
Physical Therapy
Physician
Plastics
Plumbing & Pipe Fitting
Postal Service
Printing
Property Management
Psychology
Public Health
Public Relations
Purchasing
Real Estate
Recreation & Leisure
Refrigeration & Air Conditioning
Religious Service
Restaurant
Retailing
Robotics
Sales
Secretarial
Securities
Social Science
Social Work
Speech-Language Pathology
Sports & Athletics
Sports Medicine
State & Local Government
Teaching
Technical Writing &
    Communications
Telecommunications
Telemarketing
Television & Video
Theatrical Design & Production
Tool & Die
Transportation
Travel
Trucking
Veterinary Medicine
Visual Arts
Vocational & Technical
Warehousing
Waste Management
Welding
Word Processing
Writing
Your Own Service Business

RESUMES FOR
Advertising Careers
Banking and Financial Careers
College Students &
    Recent Graduates
Communications Careers
Education Careers
Engineering Careers
Environmental Careers
Health and Medical Careers
High School Graduates
High Tech Careers
Midcareer Job Changes
Sales and Marketing Careers
Scientific and Technical Careers

 VGM Career Horizons
a division of *NTC Publishing Group*
4255 West Touhy Avenue
Lincolnwood, Illinois 60646 1975